Improve Your Spelling
Elspeth Summers

For UK order enquiries: please contact Bookpoint Ltd,
130 Milton Park, Abingdon, Oxon OX14 4SB.
Telephone: +44 (0) 1235 827720. Fax: +44 (0) 1235 400454.
Lines are open 09.00–17.00, Monday to Saturday, with a 24-hour
message answering service. Details about our titles and how to
order are available at www.teachyourself.com

Long renowned as the authoritative source for self-guided
learning – with more than 50 million copies sold worldwide –
the **Teach Yourself** series includes over 500 titles in the fields of
languages, crafts, hobbies, business, computing and education.

British Library Cataloguing in Publication Data: a catalogue record
for this title is available from the British Library.

First published in UK 2010 by Hodder Education, part of Hachette
UK, 338 Euston Road, London NW1 3BH.

This edition published 2010.

The **Teach Yourself** name is a registered trade mark of
Hodder Headline.

Copyright © 2010 Elspeth Summers

Typeset by MPS Limited, A Macmillan Company.

Printed in Great Britain for Hodder Education, an Hachette UK
Company, 338 Euston Road, London NW1 3BH, by CPI Cox &
Wyman, Reading, Berkshire RG1 8EX.

The publisher has used its best endeavours to ensure that the
URLs for external websites referred to in this book are correct and
active at the time of going to press. However, the publisher and
the author have no responsibility for the websites and can make no
guarantee that a site will remain live or that the content will remain
relevant, decent or appropriate.

Hachette UK's policy is to use papers that are natural, renewable
and recyclable products and made from wood grown in sustainable
forests. The logging and manufacturing processes are expected to
conform to the environmental regulations of the country of origin.

Impression number   10 9 8 7 6 5 4 3 2 1
Year   2014 2013 2012 2011 2010

Contents

Meet the author

Welcome to *Improve Your Spelling*!

I know that lots of people worry that their English isn't up to scratch. They are unsure when they should use 'gone' and when they should use 'went', about whether it should be 'I' or whether it should be 'me', and if it should be 'less' or if it should be 'fewer'.

But perhaps most of all, people worry about spelling. They are afraid that their spelling is letting them down, and creating a poor impression of them.

Well, as you will see in this book, spelling can be learnt, poor spelling can be improved, and everyone needs a little help from time to time. There is no shame in admitting that there are some words that simply baffle you. But there is no word that cannot be broken down, spelt out loud, practised, and committed to memory.

It just takes a little time and a bit of effort. And this book shows you how.

Elspeth Summers

Only got a minute?

The best thing you can do to improve your spelling is to read as much as possible. The more you read, the more you will become familiar with a variety of words and how they are spelt, and the more confident you will become about your own spelling.

We know from research that the shape of a word on the page plays a large part in how the brain recognizes it, so it makes sense that the more you look at words, the better you will know them. Just by becoming familiar with the shape of a word, the brain can recognize when it is spelt incorrectly, even before the actual spelling mistake is identified.

Like all skills, the skill of good spelling is one that can be improved by practice. There is no mystery to it, and everyone can do it if they take the time and follow a few simple guidelines.

The first, as I have already said, is to read, read and then read some more. The next is to be aware of some of the pitfalls of English spelling: the doubling of consonants, the silent letters and the ordering of particular vowels in certain words. If you are aware of the letter combinations that can cause problems, you will be on the lookout for them in your own writing. Also, if there are words that you repeatedly misspell, you can concentrate on getting them right, and there are various strategies you can use for this.

Finally, get into the habit of checking what you write. Don't just rely on your computer spellchecker to do it for you. Read over what you have written, paying particular attention to any problem words you have identified, and then check them in a dictionary if you are unsure of their spelling.

5 Only got five minutes?

Some of the problems that people have with English spelling are caused by words known as *homophones*. A homophone is a word that sounds like another word. It comes from Greek *homos* meaning 'same' and *phōnē* meaning 'sound'. There are three types of homophones:

1 *Homophones where the words have the same spelling but different meanings, such as* **rifle** *(the gun) and* **rifle** *(to search).*
2 *Homophones where the words have the same meaning but different spellings, such as* **cagey** *and* **cagy**.
3 *Homophones where the words have different spellings and different meanings, such as* **mist** *(a cloud of moisture in the air) and* **missed** *(the past tense of the verb 'miss').*

One of the reasons there are so many homophones in English is the fact that the sounds (or phonemes, as they are known technically) can be made by a number of letters or groups of letters. For example, a sound like 'ee' can be written in a number of ways, such as ee (as in **keep**), ea (as in **steal**), ie (as in **field**), ei (as in **protein**), e (as in **mere**), oe (as in **oestrogen**) and i (as in **naive**).

The phoneme 'sh' can be represented by sh (as in **wash**), sch (as in **schmaltz**), ch (as in **chute**), s (as in **sure**), sc (as in **fascist**), ti (as in **station**), ci (as in **acacia**), c (as in **ocean**), ss (as in **tissue**), si (as in **mansion**) and xi (as in **obnoxious**).

Many English words contain silent letters. These are letters that are not pronounced. Possibly the commonest of the silent letters is the silent e, which comes at the end of many words, such as **time**, **gate**, **note**, **life**, **fine** and **dune**.

Other silent letters include **k** in **knife**, **g** in **sign**, **l** in **walk**, **p** in **pneumonia**, **b** in **numb**, **m** in **mnemonic**, **n** in **column**, **z** in **rendezvous**, **s** in **island**, **h** in **khaki**, **d** in **handsome** and **w** in **write**.

But the presence of these oddities does not mean that English spelling cannot be learnt. There are rules to follow and strategies to implement that will allow every writer, regardless of their ability, to improve their spelling and increase their confidence in their written language.

One of the most useful methods for coping with unpredictable words is the mnemonic. A mnemonic is a line or verse that helps you remember something. It is derived from the word *mnasthai* which is Greek for 'remember'. Many of us use mnemonics without even realizing it. For example, the sentence 'Richard of York gave battle in vain' is a mnemonic for the colours of the rainbow, where the initial letter of each word matches the initial letter of each of the colours, in their correct order – red, orange, yellow, green, blue, indigo and violet.

Mnemonics can be extremely useful when learning how to spell tricky words. Here are some mnemonics for words that contain silent letters:

▶ autumn: an **u**mbrella **t**ells **u**s **m**eteorological **n**ews
▶ sign: **s**cribbling **i**ndicates **g**iven **n**ame
▶ abscess: there is a **s**cab on your ab**s**cess
▶ scene: **Sc**ott made a **sc**ary **sc**ene
▶ debt: **Deb** told me she owes a lot of money
▶ island: an island **is land** surrounded by water

By using mnemonics you can emphasize the difficult part of a word and help fix it in your mind so that spelling that word correctly becomes automatic. You can even create your own mnemonics for the words you find problematic, using names and topics that are meaningful and memorable to you.

10 Only got ten minutes?

It is generally believed that English is a hard language to learn, and that it is difficult for both native speakers and learners to get to grips with the intricacies of its spelling.

It is certainly true that the English spelling system lacks the regularity of some other languages, although it is not as completely unpredictable as is sometimes claimed. There are rules that can be followed that will apply to the majority of words, and there are also exceptions to these rules, as there are in the grammar and spelling of every language. Learning these rules will go a long way towards improving your spelling.

But what can be seen as frustrating or confusing about English spelling can also be seen as fascinating. The oddities of the English language are signs of the twists and turns it has undergone during its long and complicated development. Its history can be seen in its spelling.

English as we know it today has been close on 2000 years in the making. It takes its name from the tribe of German invaders, the Angles, who started arriving in the British Isles in the third century. The Germanic dialect spoken by these settlers formed the basis of the language that would become English. It supplanted the Celtic languages spoken by the native Britons at that time, and became established as the main language throughout most parts of what is now mainland Britain.

However, centuries of invasion, migration and borrowing have meant that the earliest form of English, Anglo-Saxon or Old English, is now as incomprehensible to a current English speaker as Old Norse or Old Icelandic. No modern-day native English speaker could read the well-known Old English poem *Beowulf* in its original form without specialist knowledge. Having said that, many words still in use in English today are derived from Old English, such as **mother** (from *modor*), **father** (*fæder*), **brother** (*brothor*), **sister** (*sweostor*), **daughter** (*dohtor*) and **son** (*sunu*). What is interesting to note about modern English words of Old English origin is that they are mainly short, with one or two syllables only, and relate to fields of human activity and experience, such as farming and raising animals (**corn, field, grass, horse** and **sheep**), the physical environment (**sea, land, tree, leaf** and **oak**), family relationships (as seen above), parts of the body (**beard, bone, eye, hair, tooth** and **nostril**), colours (**black, white, red, green** and **yellow**) and basic human functions and feelings (**love, eat, speak, thirst, eat, ache, food** and **drink**). A number of modern swear words are derived from Old English, which is why people often describe blunt, plain speaking interspersed with swearing as 'Anglo-Saxon'. This vocabulary is indicative of the core activities of the bulk of the population for hundreds of years.

While Old English formed the basis of the language we know as English, it was further supplemented by large-scale borrowing from other languages.

The first of these was Latin, initially with the arrival of Christian missionaries who brought with them the language of the new faith. Further borrowings from Latin took place at a number of later stages, continuing to the present day, as new zoological and botanical discoveries and hybrids are still given Latin names.

The next major influx of words into English came in the longboats with the Viking invaders in the eighth and ninth centuries. The Viking language – now referred to as Old Norse – contributed words such as **anger, bang, egg, ball, sky, gasp, ill** and **ugly** to English. Many places throughout the British Isles have names from Old Norse, such as **Fishguard, Cawdor, Whitby, Scunthorpe, Keswick, Ormskirk** and **Swansea**. The word **kirk**, derived from Old Norse *kirkja*, while nothing more than a place name now in England and Wales, is still alive and well in Scotland as another word for 'church', specifically a Presbyterian church, especially the Church of Scotland.

The next major influence on English started in 1066 with the Norman Conquest. Once the French conqueror William was crowned king, English became a bit of a second-class citizen as a language, standing on the sidelines while French took over as the language of the court, the aristocracy, the law, the military and the government – all the important areas, in fact. Meanwhile, English continued as the language of the ordinary people, to whom it was irrelevant if the sovereign spoke English, French or classical Latin.

This state of affairs continued until about 1400, when English began to reassert itself as the language of the royal court. Later in the century came the printing press, and with this invention the position of English as the country's foremost language was secured.

Large-scale borrowing from other languages continued, and the vocabulary of English was augmented by words from Latin and Greek, as well as from French, German, Dutch, Spanish and other European languages.

The establishment and expansion of the British Empire led to the introduction of words from languages further afield, from places such as: Africa (Swahili, Xhosa, Zulu and Afrikaans), North America (Algonquian, Inuktitut, Cree, Narrangansett and Ojibwe), Australia and New Zealand (Australian Aboriginal languages and Maori) and the Asian subcontinent (Sanskrit, Hindi, Urdu and Tamil). Trade with other countries also brought in new words from distant places (Chinese, Persian, Japanese and Arabic).

Immigration into Britain in the nineteenth, twentieth and twenty-first centuries has brought even more loan words into English, from languages such as Irish and Scottish Gaelic, Hebrew, Yiddish and Gujarati.

So what does all this borrowing mean for English spelling?
It means that English carries the influence of spelling systems from other languages all over the world. This accounts for a number of the spelling oddities in the language. These include:

▶ nouns that do not add a letter s to make the plural, such as:
phenomenon (phenomena), **bacterium** (bacteria), **stimulus**

(stimuli), **vertebra** (vertebrae), **index** (indices), **appendix** (appendices), **larynx** (larynges) and **crisis** (crises)

▶ words that contain a single letter where you might expect a double letter, such as: **aficionado, impresario, apropos, pavilion** and **millionaire**

▶ words that contain a double letter where you might expect a single letter, such as: **desiccate, innocuous, paraffin, cinnamon** and **exaggerate**

▶ words that contain unusual letter combinations, such as: **bivouac, ratatouille, diarrhoea, karaoke** and **maelstrom**

▶ words that contain silent letters, such as: **apartheid, isosceles, mortgage, yacht** and **Sikh.**

The rapid pace of technological development and the rise of the personal computer and the internet mean that words can travel round the globe more quickly than ever before. One of the great success stories of the last decade has been Wikipedia, the user-generated internet encyclopedia, which has brought a Hawaiian word into everyday English. The name Wikipedia is a combination of Hawaiian *wiki* meaning 'quick' and *encyclopedia*. 'Wiki' has now come to mean a website that allows any user to edit its content online.

And so another loan word enters the English language, not with an axe, a spear or a bible as in times past, but with the touch of a button on a keyboard. But, like its many predecessors, it comes in, settles down and makes itself at home.

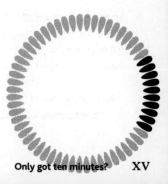

1

Who cares about spelling?

In this chapter you will learn:
- *why spelling matters*
- *how poor spelling can hamper you in your professional life*
- *how poor spelling can create a bad impression.*

You are reading this, so it would seem safe to assume that *you* care about spelling. Or you are at least interested enough to pick this book up and browse through it.

But does spelling still matter? If you are writing an email or texting a friend, you may well use a combination of abbreviations, numbers and symbols in place of full English sentences, for example: 'c u l8r' for 'See you later' and 'pub 8 sat :-)' for 'Do you want to meet me in the pub at 8 pm on Saturday? It will be fun.' Not only is this type of communication quicker, it is also cheaper, as many mobile networks charge more for longer text messages.

This kind of writing is absolutely fine between friends for gossip, jokes and making arrangements.

Insight
We all do this. You may have one style of language for talking to your friends, another for work, and another for when you have to see your child's head teacher. The technical name for this is 'style-shifting'.

Now imagine you want to write a letter to the building society to complain about the cashier who was rude and unhelpful when you went in to withdraw some money. A letter that begins 'i want 2 complain 2 u' is unlikely to be taken seriously by the person who receives it, and is less likely to achieve its aim than one that begins 'I wish to make a complaint'. Certainly, there are few adults who would think of using texting language in a formal letter and 'i want 2 complain 2 u' is probably a bit of an exaggeration. But what about a letter that begins 'I want to complain too you'? What sort of impression does it give to the person reading it? Does it really matter that 'too' should be written 'to'?

Obviously, the answer to the last question is yes. You can argue that the spelling mistake does not make any difference to the meaning of that sentence and a person reading it could overlook the error and still understand what the writer is saying. In this case that is true. After an initial surprise at reading 'too' where you expect 'to', the reader adjusts and carries on with the rest of the letter. But this is just one spelling mistake in one sentence. The reader of a 5000-word essay or 3-page letter full of spelling mistakes is likely to become more and more impatient and irritated as the mistakes pile up and the writer's meaning becomes harder to follow. If the 5000-word essay is part of an assessment for a course of training or study, the examiner is probably not going to feel very sympathetic towards the student whose essay has taken twice as long to read and mark as the rest because of all its spelling mistakes.

This may seem unfair, and many lecturers and teachers would deny that poor spelling influences them in any way, but it is a fact that if your written work has spelling mistakes, people make assumptions about you as a result.

If your spelling is not good, people often assume that you are not very intelligent. There is absolutely no evidence to connect poor spelling with low intelligence or, indeed, good spelling with high intelligence. Plenty of highly intelligent people struggle with spelling, and the list of famous poor spellers includes many high achievers such as Winston Churchill, W B Yeats, George Bernard Shaw,

Henry Ford, John F Kennedy, Albert Einstein and Benjamin Franklin. However, if the only contact a person has with you is a piece of writing that is riddled with misspellings, their impression of you is unlikely to be positive.

Insight

The English writer A A Milne once said 'My spelling is Wobbly. It's good spelling but it Wobbles, and the letters get in the wrong places.'

People might also assume that, because your letter or report is badly spelt, you are careless and probably lazy too, as you have not taken the time to check over what you have written. These assumptions, although they may be entirely false, can be difficult to dislodge.

Think of the occasions on which you have to write something that is important. Maybe you are looking for a job and have to write a covering letter, fill in an application form, sit a written aptitude test or provide a CV. You and another candidate could have identical qualifications and experience. You could both have been knowledgeable, personable and enthusiastic at the interview. But there is only one position available. What if the only real difference between you and that other applicant is the quality of the spelling in your CV? Theirs is perfect and yours is not. Many employers admit that they have rejected candidates purely because of badly spelt applications, no matter how well-qualified they were for the job. Your CV, with its spelling mistakes, allows your prospective employer to assume that you are careless, probably a bit lazy, and not very bright – and you never get the chance to prove these assumptions wrong.

Insight

A survey in 2006 showed that over three-quarters of employers were put off a candidate by poor spelling and punctuation in applications.

This is just one example of how poor spelling can be costly. There will be many times when you have to write something that needs to be just right, in order to get the result you want: a letter of complaint to a local council or your MP; a report that is to be circulated at work; a newsletter for your sports or social club; an essay for a course of study; or a letter to your child's head teacher.

If your letter or report is spelt correctly and properly punctuated with capitals and full stops, you increase the likelihood that it will be taken seriously and that people will respond to it in the way you would like.

Insight

Research done in 2008 showed that the reputation of a company could be damaged if its employees made spelling mistakes in business correspondence.

And that, after all, is the purpose of most writing: to provide the reader with information in order to evoke some kind of response. The information could be a complaint to a travel company for losing your suitcase on holiday, and the desired response is an apology and a cheque for compensation. It could be a letter to the council about the nonstop barking of the dog next door where the response would be a visit from the council's antisocial behaviour wardens. A job application is a piece of information sent in order to obtain an interview and, ultimately, a job. A newspaper article is information written in order to expand the knowledge of the readers, or to influence their opinions.

All these outcomes are made much more likely when the information presented is clearly written and correctly spelt.

Remind me: why do I need to be able to spell?

A few months ago a friend sent me a jokey email. Last week another friend sent me the same email and it occurred to me that it had a relevant point to make. Here it is, although without the photograph that accompanied the original email:

Resimay

To hoom it mae cunsern,
I waunt to apply for the job what I saw in the paper.
I can Type realee quik wit one finggar and do sum a counting.
I think I am good on the phone and I no I am a pepole person,
Pepole really seam to respond to me well. Certain men and all
the ladies. I no my spelling is not to good but find
that I Offen can get a job thru my persinalety.
My salerery is open so we can discus wat you want to pay
me and wat you think that I am werth,
I can start emeditely. Thank you in advanse fore yore anser.
hopifuly Yore best aplicant so farr.
Sinseerly,
BRYAN
PS: Because my resimay is a bit short – below is a pickture of me.

And below is a picture of an improbably handsome young man wearing nothing but a pair of swimming trunks.

Underneath Bryan's picture is the reply from his prospective employer:

Dear Bryan,
It's OK, honey, we've got a spellchecker. See you on Monday.

This email makes a number of points:

▶ *some people have too much time on their hands*
▶ *sexism is a two-way street*
▶ *most people recognize that the way you spell in an application letter will have an impact on your chances of getting the job.*

So, if you want to make a good impression the next time you put pen to paper or fingers to keyboard, and you think your spelling might be less than perfect, read on.

Insight

If you are thinking of getting a tattoo, make sure the tattooist can spell. More than one famous person has had a misspelling etched into their skin in permanent ink.

Exercise

Have a look at Bryan's résumé and see if you can correct all the mistakes in it.

10-question diagnostic test

1 *Why are you looking at this book?*
2 *Do you feel embarrassed by your spelling?*
3 *Would you like to improve your spelling?*
4 *Do you think there have been times when your spelling has let you down?*
5 *Have you ever had to write an important letter or essay?*
6 *Do you ever have to write reports or documents that are seen by a number of people?*
7 *Are you confident that the things you write create a good impression of you?*
8 *Are you trying to get your first job?*
9 *Are you trying to change jobs?*
10 *Are you trying to get a promotion at work?*

10 THINGS TO REMEMBER

1 *Poor spelling creates a poor impression.*

2 *Poor spelling can make people think you are not very bright.*

3 *Poor spelling can make people think you are a bit lazy.*

4 *Poor spelling can make people think you are careless and uninterested.*

5 *Poor spelling can make people think you would not be a good employee.*

6 *Your spelling might be the only difference between you and another candidate for a job or a promotion.*

7 *A badly spelt letter is unlikely to get the response you want.*

8 *A badly spelt letter or essay makes it difficult for the reader to understand what you mean.*

9 *A badly spelt letter or essay is likely to irritate the person reading it.*

10 *But everyone can improve their spelling if they want to.*

2

Why do people find English hard to spell?

In this chapter you will learn:
- *the reasons why English is hard to spell*
- *how the English language developed over thousands of years*
- *how many other languages contributed to English*
- *about the complex relationship between spoken sounds and written letters in English.*

In order to answer this question we need to go back more than a thousand years in time and look at the history of the English language.

A (very) brief history of English

In the third century AD, Germanic invaders started to arrive on the east coast of Britain. These invaders, the Angles, the Saxons and the Jutes, spoke dialects of a Germanic language. At that time the native British population spoke various Celtic languages. As these Germanic speakers came in greater numbers and settled, the Celtic languages gradually died out throughout Britain, apart from in a few areas in the north and west, where they survived – Cornwall and parts of Wales and Scotland. The Germanic language took over.

We know this language as Anglo-Saxon, and it takes its name from two of the invading Germanic tribes, the Angles and the Saxons. Anglo-Saxon, or Old English as it is also known, was the language spoken throughout most of England until the eleventh century.

There are many words from Anglo-Saxon still in use today in English. Typically, these words are short, with only one or two syllables, and they are the words that relate to the most essential of human concerns and activities, such as family, the physical environment, the parts of the body, colours, farm animals and agriculture, for example:

ache	father	mother
acorn	field	mouse
axe	food	
	foot	name
bath	friend	nostril
beard		
beer	gather	oak
bird	grass	orchard
blood	green	
bone		plant
brother	hair	plough
	hammer	
child	hill	queen
cold	horse	
corn		rain
cow	king	rat
	knife	red
daughter		roof
dead	lamb	
dog	land	salt
drunk	leaf	sea
	love	sheep
eat		sister
empty	man	speak
eye	meat	storm

sword	udder	wolf
		woman
thing	walk	
thirst	warm	yellow
tooth	water	yolk
tree	white	

> **Insight**
>
> Because many of the swear words still used in English
> today are from Old English, people still refer to blunt,
> straightforward language peppered with swearing as
> 'Anglo-Saxon'.

The first large-scale wave of borrowing into English came about
with the introduction of Christianity into the country, and Latin
supplied the new vocabulary needed to serve this new religion.

This borrowing was followed by an influx of Old Norse words in
the eighth and ninth centuries, brought in by Viking invaders from
Scandinavia who then settled in the villages and towns they had
captured.

These new words were absorbed and Anglo-Saxon continued to
be the language of both formal and everyday life. This situation
changed dramatically in 1066.

In October the English king, Harold, was defeated by William,
Duke of Normandy, at Hastings, and on Christmas Day William
was crowned King of England at Westminster.

With the arrival of a French king and his French nobles and
courtiers, Anglo-Saxon was shoved aside as the language of
officialdom, and had to make way for Old Norman, William's
native tongue. For the next 300 years, English (now in its Middle
English phase) was the language of the common people only. The
French of the court combined with a little Old English created a
language we now call Anglo-Norman and this was the language of
law, government, learning, military matters, culture and society.
During this time a huge number of French words came into

English, and these words reflect the different functions of Anglo-Norman and English. The words for animals that were farmed and hunted were from Anglo-Saxon: **cow, pig, deer** and **sheep**. By the time the animal had reached the dining table it was going by a French name: **beef, pork, venison** and **mutton**.

From around 1400 onwards, English was starting to re-establish itself as the language of the ruling classes. The last quarter of the fifteenth century is considered to mark the end of Middle English and the beginning of Early Modern English. In 1475 William Caxton produced the first printed book in English, *The Recuyell of the Histories of Troye*, Caxton's own translation of a French work. The following year he set up his printing press in London and produced the first edition of Chaucer's *Canterbury Tales*.

The arrival of printing was fundamental to the re-establishment of English as *the* language in England. The start of mass communication depended on the use of the language that most people spoke: English.

One other very important thing started in the time of Early Modern English, although it took over 300 years to finish. This is the change known as the Great Vowel Shift. It was a gradual changing of how certain vowels were pronounced. This is a hugely complicated subject and a spelling book could not – and should not – begin to explain its causes or effects. However, the Great Vowel Shift still has an impact on spelling today. This is because the spelling and the pronunciation of English once corresponded closely. That is, the words were spelt the way they sounded. The standardization of English spelling did not come about till after the invention of printing – it simply wasn't needed before. But as English spelling was being standardized and fixed, its pronunciation was starting to change (because of the Great Vowel Shift) and by the time the pronunciation had stopped changing, the way English was written was no longer the way English was said.

And that is just one of the reasons that English spelling can be so difficult to learn.

Words from other languages

As we have seen, languages such as Latin, Old Norse and Old
Norman French have contributed thousands of words to English.
And these languages are not alone in that. Chapter 11 shows just
how welcoming English has been to thousands of words from
dozens of languages, and this receptiveness continues to this day.
But these words bring their own problems for the writer of English.
Other languages have their own spelling rules and, yes, oddities.
This means that an English speller is having to contend with words
from all over the world, some of which become plural in different
ways, have single letters where you might expect a double letter,
have double letters where you might expect a single letter, have
unusual letter combinations and have accents that do not exist in
English. No wonder we get confused.

Sounds the same

The technical term for a word that sounds the same as another
word is a **homophone**, from Greek *homos*, meaning 'same', and
phōnē, meaning 'voice' or 'sound'. English has many pairs (for
example **peer** and **pier**) and triplets (for example **rain** and **reign**
and **rein**) and even quartets (for example **right** and **rite** and **write**
and **wright**) of homophones, and these can cause understandable
confusion for the writer. See Chapter 8 for a lot more information
about homophones and how to disentangle them.

English sounds versus English letters

We have already seen how the Great Vowel Shift contributed to
the mismatch between English spelling and English pronunciation.
But there were other factors involved.

Anglo-Saxon had been written in runes before the introduction of the Roman alphabet by Christian missionaries. But there were not enough Roman letters to represent all the sounds, so this led to some combining of letters. During the Middle English period, when Anglo-Norman was in the ascendancy, French scribes introduced some new characters into the alphabet: **k**, **g**, **q**, **v**, **w** and **z**. The letter **k**, for example, was introduced in order to represent the hard 'k' sound at the beginning of words like **keep**, which is from Anglo-Saxon *cepan*, meaning 'to observe'. This was to allow a distinction to be made between this sound and the 'ch' sound at the beginning of words like **chicken**, which is from Anglo-Saxon *cicen*. Unfortunately, this was not done consistently, so English retains words like **clean**, **cold** and **cup**, all of which are from Anglo-Saxon, and all of which have the initial hard 'k' sound but are spelt with the letter **c**.

Two Anglo-Saxon letters, ð (which is called 'eth') and þ (which is called 'thorn'), were replaced by the letters **th**.

Insight

It is an incorrect reading of the letter thorn (þ) as y in the word the (þe) that has given rise to the use of ye as a supposedly archaic form of the, as in *Ye Olde Tea Shoppe*.

ONE SOUND, MANY LETTERS

Now let's take a look at how some English sounds can be spelt in more than one way.

VOWELS

The following groups of words all contain the same vowel sounds:

name, aid, rein, pare, wear, hair, heir, fairy
grass, path, palm, harm, heart, clerk
sat, bad, have, marry
lean, keel, chief, seize, gear, sheer, here, bier, query

red, said, thread, bury
side, shy, dye, height, hire, byre, fiery
pin, busy, hymn, women
bone, road, foe, low, dough
haul, lawn, fall, bought, swarm, more, soar, floor, port, Tory
got, shot, shone
fool, soup, boor, tour
good, full, would
tune, due, newt, view, endure, fury
bud, run, love
heard, bird, word, absurd
mount, frown, sour
toy, boy, soil

Exercise

The missing words in each of the following sentences all have the same
vowel sound. Can you work out what they should be?

1 The r___ in S___ falls m___ on the p___.
2 I will need r__ t___ to finish sewing this b__s___, she s___.
3 Have you h___ that a___ B___ Song that they always play
   at weddings?
4 I l___ to r___ along the beach before the s___ is u_.
5 The c___ r___ for being h__ is to drink all your b___.

CONSONANTS

The following groups of words all contain the same
consonant sounds:

b	hob, rabbit
ch	church, much, match
d	ado, dhal, teddy
f	faint, if, puff, phase, rough
g	gold, rugged, guard, ghastly
h	happy, home
j	jack, adjective, soldier, gentle, ledge, region
k	keep, cat, chorus, mucky

kw	question, coiffure
l	lamp, collar
m	meat, palm, stammer
n	net, gnome, pneumonia, mnemonic, knee, dinner
p	peat, apple
r	rest, wreck, arrive, rhyme
s	sad, city, scene, mass, psalm, receive, tsunami
sh	shine, machine, sure, station, acacia, issue, ocean, conscious, obnoxious, tension, schedule
t	tape, nettle, thyme, right, debt, indict
v	valid, river, Weimar
w	was, one, twig
y	young, bastion
z	zoo, was, roads, fuzz, tsar, czar
zh	azure, measure, lesion

Exercise

The missing words in the following sentences all have the same consonant sound. Can you work out what they should be? The sound is shown in brackets at the end of each example.

1 Did you r___ the p___ I sent? It was the DVD of S__ and the C___. ('s' sound)
2 He was feeling e___ a___ because he knew that the c___ interview with the N___ Trust was s___ for the next day. ('sh' sound)
3 It's no f__ when you have a c___ and you can't get any medicine because the p___ closed at h___ past one. ('f' sound)
4 Trying to explain the pension s___ to you is l___ t___ to a b___ wall. ('k' sound)
5 The d___ passed by in a h___ of b___ and parties. ('z' sound)

Silent letters

The last big problem with English spelling is the issue of its silent letters. It has been suggested that each of English's 26 letters can be silent in at least one word. Here are some words with silent letters:

a   spread, earth
b   debt, lamb
c   muscle, indict
d   handsome, handkerchief
e   mole, live
f   halfpenny
g   gnome, align
h   honest, ghost
i   business
k   knee, knife
l   calf, walk
m   mnemonic
n   column, autumn
o   jeopardy, leopard
p   psychiatry, receipt
q   racquet
r   February
s   aisle, island
t   thistle, ballet
u   guest, guilt
w   answer, wrong
x   faux
y   say, prey
z   chez, rendezvous

Insight

The silent b in **debt** has never been pronounced. The original word was *dette* and the b was added because of influence from Latin *dēbitum*. However, the k at the start of **knee** and **knife** *was* originally pronounced.

Exercise

Insert the missing words in the following sentences. Each word contains a silent letter and the first letter of the word is shown, just to get you started.

1 Everyone k___ that George Clooney is a h___ man.
2 In days of old, k___ may have been bold, but they still carried their s___ everywhere.
3 Last W___ we went to London to see the s___. My favourites were Nelson's C___ and the River T___.
4 Tying a k___ in your h___ is supposed to help you remember things.
5 When the t___ hit the i___, a huge wave destroyed the houses, leaving d___ everywhere.
6 I w___ like smoked s___ and a glass of c___.
7 Dame M___ Fonteyn earned great f___ as a b___ dancer.
8 I had p___ the w___ of last a___ and it was C___ before I was completely better.
9 It's none of your d___ b___ how I spend my money!

One well-known proponent of English spelling reform, the playwright George Bernard Shaw, is alleged to have claimed that the word **fish** might as well be written **ghoti** in English. The 'f' sound is written as **gh** in words like **rough** and **cough**. The 'i' sound is written as **o** in **women**. And the 'sh' sound is written as **ti** in words like **nation** and **election**. So, according to its sound, it could be **gh + o + ti = ghoti**.

Insight

Following this reasoning, **fish** could also be spelt **phech** (the 'f' sound from **photograph**, the 'i' sound from **pretty** and the 'sh' sound from **machine**).

Spelling reform

For all the reasons just mentioned, many people, including George Bernard Shaw, have campaigned over the years for the simplification of English spelling.

Suggestions for the reform of English spelling were first made in the sixteenth century, and numerous schemes have been proposed in the years since then, none of which have enjoyed any real degree of success or popular support.

The proposals may vary in their detail and scope, but they centre on the idea of bringing English spelling and English pronunciation closer together. A simplified, phonetic system is at the core of every plan to reform English spelling.

However, the problems facing these plans are many. These are just a few of them:

> *English has too few letters and too many sounds to have a straight, one-to-one relationship between the letter and the sound.*
> *There is strong resistance to the idea of spelling reform.*
> *There is no official body that is 'in charge' of the English language which can authorize, or even champion, a system of spelling reform.*
> *There are so many regional accents in the UK alone – which accent would a reformed phonetic system be based on?*
> *It would be unbelievably expensive to implement a new system of spelling.*

Many languages have implemented spelling reforms at different points in their history. These include Dutch, Norwegian, Portuguese and Spanish. In recent years, both French and German have undergone spelling reform. In Germany, the reforms introduced in 1998 were the result of almost 20 years of discussion. The reforms have been widely opposed and surveys suggest that a majority of the German-speaking population are still reluctant to accept the new spellings.

Insight

In German, all nouns begin with a capital letter. It was suggested that this convention be abolished but this was rejected and the initial capitals remain. It sometimes appears that British English is moving in that direction with the spread of Random Capitalization (see Chapter 5).

All this goes to show that to reform a spelling system is no small task. It takes a lot of discussion, determination, planning and, perhaps most importantly, money to carry it out.

In the case of the English language, the movement towards the reform of its spelling remains very much on the outskirts of mainstream politics, and without any driving force behind it, it carries no real weight with most native English speakers. If the German example is anything to go by, even if the current government decided tomorrow that English spelling reform was its number one priority, it could be 2030 before any law to that effect was passed, and then who knows how much longer before the legal wrangling ended.

English spelling as it is right now is here to stay.

So let's get to work!

10-question diagnostic test

1 When did the first Germanic invaders come to Britain?
2 Which tribes were they?
3 Which languages were the native British people speaking at that time?
4 This Germanic language is known by two names. What are they?
5 Why did Latin words first enter English?
6 How did Old Norse words come into English?
7 Which language did William the Conqueror speak?
8 What was the important language change that started around 1450?
9 What happened in 1475 that was important in the history of English?
10 Which two Anglo-Saxon letters were replaced by the letters 'th'?

10 THINGS TO REMEMBER

1 *The language we speak today is the result of over 1800 years of development.*

2 *For 300 years of its history English was not the most important language spoken in the British Isles.*

3 *The standardization of spelling came about as a result of the invention of the printing press.*

4 *Spelling was standardized at the point when English pronunciation was still changing, so spelling and pronunciation are often not obviously connected.*

5 *Dozens of languages have contributed words to English.*

6 *English has many homophones.*

7 *The English language has more sounds than it has letters to express them.*

8 *Many English sounds can be made by more than one letter or combination of letters.*

9 *Almost every letter in the alphabet can be silent in at least one word.*

10 *Spelling reform is many years away.*

3

How can I improve my spelling?

In this chapter you will learn:
- *about the importance of reading as an aid to spelling*
- *some simple techniques to help improve your spelling*
- *how to use the five-step spelling programme to perfect your spelling.*

The good news is that there are lots of things you can do to improve your spelling. The first one below may seem obvious but it's impossible to overestimate its importance.

The three r's

In this context the three r's are – read, read and read. Reading is absolutely fundamental to becoming a better speller. The more you read, the more familiar you become with a wide variety of words. Words that puzzled you the first time you saw them become easier to read, recognize and remember. Research has shown that a large part of how we recognize a word is based on the shape its letters make. So, if you see the word repeatedly, you recognize how it *ought* to look. If the word is spelt incorrectly, you are likely to have a feeling that something is wrong with the way it is written, even before you look closely enough to examine the mistake.

Reading widens your vocabulary and helps to fix the words you already know in your mind. If you come across an unfamiliar word, try to work out what it means from the words around it. Then look it up in a dictionary. Does the meaning given make sense in what you have been reading? Say the word out loud. Write it down. Keep a notebook for any unknown words you encounter in the course of your reading. An address book is useful for this, as you can enter the words under their initial letter. Or put them in your mobile phone or personal organizer. You should always be alert for new and unfamiliar words. Practise spelling them (there is more on this later in the chapter). Once you feel confident about them, why not try and use them in your own speech or writing?

Insight

You probably used to do this at school. The teacher would give the class a list of words and for homework you had to put each one into a sentence. It's a useful exercise for checking if you understand what each word means and how it is used.

What should you read? Read whatever interests you – newspapers, magazines, football programmes, comics, novels, biographies, the TV listings – whatever. Reading should never be a chore, so don't beat yourself up because you take *Heat* magazine on the train instead of *War and Peace*. And once you've finished *Heat*, read the adverts and the notices on the train, or the bus, or on the billboards when you stop at traffic lights. The point is to try to imprint as many words as you can in your memory so that spelling them correctly becomes automatic. Whenever you are reading, you are doing something to improve your spelling, whether you are reading Tolstoy or *Motorcycle Monthly*.

Insight

According to statistics, over 133,000 new books were published in Britain in 2009. There are around 100 daily newspapers and about 2,800 monthly magazines for a general, rather than a specialized, readership. Somewhere there is something of interest for every reader.

Break it down now

When you are writing a word, you might find it helpful to break it into sections in your mind.

In a previous job, I had to do a lot of proofreading. I was often asked to proofread covers for dictionaries. There can be few worse places for an uncaught spelling mistake than a dictionary cover. It is generally considered that a misspelt word in the title of a dictionary undermines the book's authority.

One of the methods I used when proofreading was breaking each word down into smaller sections as I read it, for example:

SOMEONE'S ENGLISH DICTIONARY:
   This is an indispensable tool for any lover of language

In my head (and under my breath) I would sound this out as:

SOME + ONE'S ENG + LISH DIC + TION + ARY:
   This is an in + dis + pens + able tool for any lov + er of lang + uage

This method is particularly useful for words that have silent letters, for example:

Wednesday	Wed + nes + day	**definite**	def + in + ite
secretary	sec + ret + ary	**government**	gov + ern + ment
February	Feb + ru + ary		

You may also find that it helps when you break the word down to say the sections to yourself, sounding out every bit. It can also help if you exaggerate the pronunciation when you do it, especially if the spelling and the normal pronunciation are far enough apart to cause problems, for example:

separate	sep + ar + ate
laboratory	lab + or + a + tor + y

Doing this should help you remember any letters that are not pronounced and should also reinforce the look of the word in your mind.

A word within a word

When you are looking at a word, try to see if there are any smaller words contained within the word, for example **calendar** contains the word **lend**. Some other examples of this are:

Word	Word contained
acquit	**quit**
amateur	**mate**
bargain	**gain**
cemetery	**meter**
colonel	**lone**
dependent	**end**
environment	**iron**
extrovert	**rove**
foreign	**reign**
gorgeous	**gorge**
identity	**dent**
inadvertent	**advert**
leisure	**sure**
luminescent	**mine** and **scent**
miscellaneous	**cell**
neurosis	**euro**
outrageous	**rage**
phlegm	**leg**
Protestant	**pro** and **test** and **ant**
refrigerator	**rig**
sausage	**usage**
soliloquy	**lilo**
tragedy	**raged**
vegetarian	**get**
warrant	**war** and **rant**

Insight

The **g** in **phlegm** is silent because when the word was
originally used in the fifteenth century it was *fleume*, which
was an Old French word. However, in the course of the
sixteenth century the spelling changed to be closer to the
original Greek form, which was *phlegma*. But the original
pronunciation remained.

Exercise

Look through the list of problem words in Chapter 6 and see how many
smaller words you can find within them.

Only connect

English is full of groups of words that come from the same root
and so have similar spelling patterns. When you see a word,
try of think of a word that it is related to. If you can spot these
connections between words, it will help you remember how to spell
them, for example:

arbitrary and *arbitrate*
benefit and *beneficial*
continue and *continuous* and *continual*
define and *definite*
disciple and *discipline*
family and *familiar*
luminous and *luminescent*
minus and *minuscule*
muscle and *muscular*
medical and *medicine*
oppose and *opponent*
phlegm and *phlegmatic*
practical and *practice*
profess and *profession*
puberty and *pubescent*

reserve and *reservoir*
sign and *signature*
vehicle and *vehicular*

> ## Insight
>
> This technique is particularly useful for words with silent
> letters. Often, a letter that is silent in one word is pronounced
> in another word that is related to it, for example **muscle** and
> **muscular**, **sign** and **signature** and **vehicle** and **vehicular**.

Chapter 7 of this book tells you a lot more about root words in
English and their meanings.

Check it out now

Get into the habit of rereading everything you have written. If there
are any words you are not sure about, check them in a dictionary.
This is as important in a business email or a personal letter as it is
for the cover of a dictionary. Once again, it is about the impression
of you that your writing gives.

If you are filling in an application for a job or writing your CV,
leave yourself enough time for this stage, so that you can read it
over carefully. If there is someone whose spelling you trust, ask
them to read it as well, and make a note of any words you have
got wrong. Be sure to add these words to your own personal list
of problem words. Recognizing that you are unsure of how a
particular word is spelt is an important part of becoming a better
speller. If you know that you always have problems with 'privilege'
(as I do), then you will take time to think about it when you have
to write it. And then check it in the dictionary.

> ## Insight
>
> A word of warning: this can lead to proofreader's disease, in
> which the sufferer obsessively checks everything they read,
> becomes agitated when they find errors and, in extreme cases,
> corrects spelling mistakes on menus and notices.

The five-step spelling programme

There is a famous quotation that is often ascribed to the hugely successful American golfer Arnold Palmer, although whether he is actually its originator is uncertain. According to legend, someone called him 'lucky' and he replied with the line: 'Yes, and the more I practise, the luckier I get'. (Although, being American, Palmer would obviously have said 'practice' rather than 'practise'.)

That is where the similarity between being a good speller and being a world-class professional golfer begin and end. People are no more born good spellers than they are born great golfers. A person may have a natural ability for one or the other (or even both!) but everyone needs to practise and with practice comes confidence and, sometimes, skill.

So here is a five-step plan for perfecting your spelling.

STEP ONE: READ

Look closely at the word. Look at it letter by letter. Break it into sections as described above. For example:

privilege   **p + r + i + v + i + l + e + g + e**   **pri + vil + ege**

STEP TWO: SAY

Say the word out loud. Also say it in an exaggerated way, pronouncing all the letters, even any silent ones. Say it in its sections as well.

STEP THREE: COVER

Cover the word over. Try to remember how it looks. See if you can spell it in your head or out loud.

STEP FOUR: WRITE

Now, without looking at the word again, write it down.

STEP FIVE: CHECK

Check your spelling of the word against the original. Are they the same? If so, well done. If not, go back to step one and try again until you spell it correctly.

You can try this method with some of the problem words in Chapter 6. Every so often it is worth going back to try a few you think you know already, just to be sure they're still firmly fixed in your mind.

10-question diagnostic test

1 *What is the best thing you can do to improve your spelling?*
2 *What has research shown about the way that we recognize individual words?*
3 *Can you suggest three places to record any new words you come across?*
4 *Which technique are you using when you see the word* **science** *within* **conscience**?
5 *Which technique are you using when you see the word* **muscle** *and it makes you think of the word* **muscular**?
6 *Which technique are you using when you look at the word* **acknowledgement** *and read it out to yourself as* **ac + know + ledge + ment**?
7 *What should you do every time you write something?*
8 *What else can you do if, for example, you are writing something important like an application for a job?*
9 *What do you do when you have to write a word that you know you have got wrong in the past?*
10 *What are the five steps of the five-step spelling programme?*

10 THINGS TO REMEMBER

1   *Everyone can improve their spelling.*

2   *The best thing you can do to improve your spelling is read, read, read.*

3   *Get into the habit of writing down any new words you come across and making sure you know what they mean and how to spell them.*

4   *When you are writing a word, break it into sections in your mind.*

5   *Say those sections out loud when you look at the word.*

6   *Exaggerate the pronunciation, and pronounce any silent letters.*

7   *Look for smaller words within words when you are writing.*

8   *Think in terms of groups of words – which other words are connected to the one you are writing?*

9   *Check everything you have written and, if necessary, ask someone else to look over it.*

10 *Use the five-step spelling programme to learn new words: read, say, cover, write, check.*

4

....

What are the rules?

In this chapter you will learn:
- *about the function of suffixes in English*
- *how word endings change when suffixes are added*
- *about the 'i before e except after c' rule*
- *whether to use ise or ize.*

You may be surprised to learn that there are not that many rules in English spelling. The best thing to do is to become familiar with the regular rules, and feel confident about them, and then look at the exceptions, of which there are only a few. Use this chapter as a reference whenever you are not certain.

Most English spelling rules relate to the addition of suffixes to basic words. A suffix is a letter or group of letters added to the end of an existing word to make another word, for example:

dog + **s** = *dogs*
faint + **ed** = *fainted*
yellow + **est** = *yellowest*
sad + **ness** = *sadness*

Suffixes are added for a number of reasons. If you understand how certain types of word behave when a suffix is added, then you understand most of the rules of English spelling!

What are the suffixes?

Suffixes perform a number of functions in English:

▶ *to make a singular noun plural: add* s *or* es
▶ *to make a comparative form of an adjective: add* er
▶ *to make a superlative form of an adjective: add* est
▶ *to make the third person singular present tense of a verb:*
  add s *or* es
▶ *to make the present participle of a verb: add* ing
▶ *to make the past tense of a verb: add* d *or* ed
▶ *to make a derived form of a word: add* ness, ism, dom, less,
  ful, y, ly, *and so on.*

How a word behaves when a suffix is added to it depends on the word's final letter or letters. The following sections are arranged in this way, by the final letter or letters of the word.

Word endings a–z

WORDS THAT END WITH THE LETTER A

▶ *plural noun – add* s: *umbrella* + s = *umbrellas*
▶ *third person singular – add* s: *henna* + s = *hennas*
▶ *present participle – add* ing: *henna* + ing = *hennaing*
▶ *past tense – add* ed: *henna* + ed = *hennaed*
▶ *derived form – add* suffix: *bra* + less = *braless*

WORDS THAT END WITH THE LETTER B

▶ *plural noun – add* s: *job* + s = *jobs*
▶ *comparative – add* er: *dumb* + er = *dumber*
▶ *superlative – add* est: *numb* + est = *numbest*
▶ *third person singular – add* s: *climb* + s = *climbs*

- *present participle – add* **ing**: *climb +* **ing** *= climbing*
- *past tense – add* **ed**: *climb +* **ed** *= climbed*
- *derived form – add* **suffix**: *herb +* **y** *= herby*

Exceptions: for some adjectives and verbs that end in a **b**, you double the **b** before adding **er, est, ing** and **ed**. These are adjectives and verbs of one syllable that end with a single vowel followed by **b**; and also verbs of more than one syllable that end with a single short vowel followed by **b**, in which the stress is on the end of the word. If a one-syllable word ends with a short vowel followed by a **b**, you double the **b** before adding a suffix that begins with a vowel or the letter **y**:

drab → *drabb + er = drabber*
glib → *glibb + est = glibbest*
stab → *stabb + ing = stabbing*
fib → *fibb + ed = fibbed*
demob → *demobb + ing = demobbing*
demob → *demobb + ed = demobbed*
club → *clubb + able = clubbable*
snob → *snobb + y = snobby*

WORDS THAT END WITH THE LETTER C

- *plural noun – add* **s**: *attic +* **s** *= attics*
- *comparative – add* **er**: *chic +* **er** *= chicer*
- *superlative – add* **est**: *chic +* **est** *= chicest*
- *third person singular – add* **s**: *picnic +* **s** *= picnics*
- *present participle – add* **k** *before adding* **ing**: *mimic →*
  mimick + **ing** *= mimicking*
- *past tense – add* **k** *before adding* **ed**: *panic → panick +* **ed**
  = panicked
- *derived form: add* **k** *before adding* **suffix**: *traffic → traffick*
  + er = trafficker; garlic → garlick + y = garlicky

Exceptions: the verbs **arc** (to form an arc) and **sync** (to synchronize) do not take a **k** before adding **ing** or **ed**; if you add the suffix **able** to **traffic**, you do not add a **k**:

arc + **ing** = *arcing*
sync + **ed** = *synced*
traffic + **able** = *trafficable*

WORDS THAT END WITH THE LETTER D

▶ *plural noun – add* **s***: hand* + **s** = *hands*
▶ *comparative – add* **er***: loud* + **er** = *louder*
▶ *superlative – add* **est***: grand* + **est** = *grandest*
▶ *third person singular – add* **s***: breed* + **s** = *breeds*
▶ *present participle – add* **ing***: land* + **ing** = *landing*
▶ *past tense – add* **ed***: flood* + **ed** = *flooded*
▶ *derived form – add* **suffix***: command* + **ment** = *commandment*;
  wind + **y** = *windy*

Exceptions: for some adjectives and verbs that end in a **d**, you double the **d** before adding er, est, ing and ed. These are adjectives and verbs of one syllable that end with a single vowel followed by **d**; and also verbs of more than one syllable that end with a single short vowel followed by **d**, in which the stress is on the end of the word. If a one-syllable word ends with a short vowel followed by a **d**, you double the **d** before adding a suffix beginning with a vowel or the letter **y**; if a word has more than one syllable and ends with a single short vowel followed by **d** and the stress is on the end of the word, then you double the **d** before adding a suffix beginning with a vowel or y:

sad → *sadd* + **er** = *sadder*
red → *redd* + **est** = *reddest*
nod → *nodd* + **ing** = *nodding*
thud → *thudd* + **ed** = *thudded*
forbid → *forbidd* + **ing** = *forbidding*
embed → *embedd* + **ed** = *embedded*
bid → *bidd* + **er** = *bidder*
mud → *mudd* + **y** = *muddy*
outbid → *outbidd* + **er** = *outbidder*

WORDS THAT END WITH THE LETTER E

▸ *plural noun – add* **s**: *fee +* **s** *= fees*
▸ *comparative – add* **r**: *rude +* **r** *= ruder*
▸ *superlative – add* **st**: *wee +* **st** *= weest*
▸ *third person singular – add* **s**: *adore +* **s** *= adores*
▸ *present participle – drop the final* **e** *and then add* **ing**:
   like → lik + **ing** *= liking*
▸ *past tense – add* **d**: *phone +* **d** *= phoned*
▸ *derived form – see below*

Exceptions: three very common nouns ending with the letters **fe** do not make their plurals in the usual way. For these you change the **f** to **v** and then add an **s** after the final **e**:

knife → knive + **s** *= knives*
life → live + **s** *= lives*
wife → wive + **s** *= wives*

Exceptions: the present participle of most words ending in **e** is created by dropping the final **e** before adding **ing**. There are a few groups of exceptions.

If a verb ends with **ee, ie, oe** or **ye**, you just add **ing**, without dropping the final **e**:

agree + **ing** *= agreeing*
boogie + **ing** *= boogieing*
canoe + **ing** *= canoeing*
dye + **ing** *= dyeing*
eye + **ing** *= eyeing*

But, take note of the following common verbs, which have their own rules when adding **ing**: for **die, lie, tie** and **vie**, you change the **i** to **y**, drop the **e** and then add **ing**:

die → dy + **ing** *= dying*
lie → ly + **ing** *= lying*

tie → *ty* + **ing** = *tying*
vie → *vy* + **ing** = *vying*

Derived form: if a word ends with a silent **e**, you drop this **e** before adding a suffix that begins with a vowel or the suffix **y**:

collapse → *collaps* + **ible** = *collapsible*
create → *creat* + **ion** = *creation*
bone → *bon* + **y** = *bony*
grease → *greas* + **y** = *greasy*

Exceptions: if a word ends with the letters **ce** and this sounds like letter **s**, or if it ends with the letters **ge** and this sounds like letter **j**, you do not drop the final **e** before adding a suffix that begins with a vowel:

service + **able** = *serviceable*
courage + **ous** = *courageous*

If a suffix begins with a consonant, it can be added to the word without any other change being made:

apprentice + **ship** = *apprenticeship*

Exceptions: although most words drop the final **e** before adding the suffix **y**, there are some words that can be done in two different ways, either with the final **e** or without it; neither is considered to be wrong though the most common is shown first:

dope → *dopey* or *dopy*
game → *gamey* or *gamy*
home → *homey* or *homy*
horse → *horsy* or *horsey*
mange → *mangy* or *mangey*
mouse → *mousy* or *mousey*
nose → *nosey* or *nosy*
price → *pricey* or *pricy*
smile → *smiley* or *smily*
stage → *stagey* or *stagy*

The adjective created by adding **hole** and the suffix **y**, meaning 'full of holes', is **holey**. As you can see, the **e** is kept in this word, most likely to distinguish it from the adjective **holy** which means 'sacred'.

In order to make an adverb from an adjective you generally add the suffix **ly**:

stupid + **ly** = *stupidly*

But when the adjective ends with the letters **le**, the rule is different. For these adjectives you replace the final **e** with **y**:

horrible → *horribly*
subtle → *subtly*

Exception: to make an adverb from the adjective **whole**, you drop the final **e** and then add **ly**:

whole → *whol* + **ly** = *wholly*

WORDS THAT END WITH THE LETTER F

▶ *plural noun – add* **s**: *bailiff* + **s** = *bailiffs*
▶ *comparative – add* **er**: *gruff* + **er** = *gruffer*
▶ *superlative – add* **est**: *bluff* + **est** = *bluffest*
▶ *third person singular – add* **s**: *stuff* + **s** = *stuffs*
▶ *present participle – add* **ing**: *stuff* + **ing** = *stuffing*
▶ *past tense – add* **ed**: *stuff* + **ed** = *stuffed*
▶ *derived form – add* **suffix**: *roof* + **less** = *roofless*;
  huff + **y** = *huffy*

Exceptions: there are a number of nouns ending with **f** that are made plural by changing the **f** to **v** and adding **es**, for example:

aardwolf → *aardwolv* + **es** = *aardwolves*
calf → *calv* + **es** = *calves*

elf → *elv* + **es** = *elves*
leaf → *leav* + **es** = *leaves*
loaf → *loav* + **es** = *loaves*
self → *selv* + **es** = *selves*
sheaf → *sheav* + **es** = *sheaves*
shelf → *shelv* + **es** = *shelves*
thief → *thiev* + **es** = *thieves*
werewolf → *werewolv* + **es** = *werewolves*
wolf → *wolv* + **es** = *wolves*
yourself → *yourselv* + **es** = *yourselves*

Insight

The word **staff** is an interesting one when it comes to plurals.
When **staff** has the meaning of 'a stick' or 'a set of lines on
which music is written', it can have one of two plurals: **staffs**
or **staves**. When it means 'a group of people employed in an
organization', the plural is always **staffs**.

There is also a group of nouns that end with a single letter **f**. These
are the words that can have either the **s** or **ves** plural although, in
most cases, one is much commoner than the other. These are listed
below, with the most common plural first:

dwarf → *dwarfs* or *dwarves*
half → *halves* or *halfs*
hoof → *hooves* or *hoofs*
oaf → *oafs* or *oaves*
scarf → *scarves* or *scarfs*
turf → *turfs* or *turves*
wharf → *wharves* or *wharfs*

Insight

The correct plural of **dwarf** is one that causes debate.
Historically **dwarfs** is the plural, as in the Disney film *Snow
White and the Seven Dwarfs*. But **dwarves**, which had been a
rare alternative since the eighteenth century, was popularized
by the work of JRR Tolkein, supposedly as a parallel to

(Contd)

the plural **elves**. **Dwarfs** is generally used for people with dwarfism and for the astronomical stars, such as blue and red dwarfs, while **dwarves** is used for the mythical creatures.

WORDS THAT END WITH THE LETTER G

▶ *plural noun – add* **s**: *frog* + **s** = *frogs*
▶ *comparative – add* **er**: *long* + **er** = *longer*
▶ *superlative – add* **est**: *long* + **est** = *longest*
▶ *third person singular – add* **s**: *dig* + **s** = *digs*
▶ *present participle – add* **ing**: *hang* + **ing** = *hanging*
▶ *past tense – add* **ed**: *bang* + **ed** = *banged*
▶ *derived form – add* **suffix**: *king* + **dom** = *kingdom*

Exceptions: for some adjectives and verbs that end in **g**, you double the **g** before adding **er**, **est**, **ing** and **ed**. These are adjectives and verbs of one syllable that end with a single vowel followed by **g**; and also verbs of more than one syllable that end with a single short vowel followed by **g**, in which the stress is on the end of the word. If a one-syllable word ends with a short vowel followed by a **g**, you double the **g** before adding a suffix beginning with a vowel or letter **y**; if a word has more than one syllable and ends with a single short vowel followed by **g** and the stress is on the end of the word, then you double the **g** before adding a suffix beginning with a vowel or **y**:

big → bigg + **er** = *bigger*
big → bigg + **est** = *biggest*
hug → hugg + **ing** = *hugging*
hug → hugg + **able** = *huggable*
fog → fogg + **y** = *foggy*
peg → pegg + **ed** = *pegged*
debug → debugg + **er** = *debugger*
debug → debugg + **ed** = *debugged*
unplug → unplugg + **ing** = *unplugging*

WORDS THAT END WITH THE LETTER H

▶ *plural noun – add* **s**: *cheetah* + **s** = *cheetahs*
▶ *comparative – add* **er**: *rich* + **er** = *richer*

- *superlative – add* **est**: *high +* **est** *= highest*
- *third person singular – add* **s**: *aah +* **s** *= aahs*
- *present participle – add* **ing**: *sigh +* **ing** *= sighing*
- *past tense – add* **ed**: *froth +* **ed** *= frothed*
- *derived form – add* **suffix**: *death +* **like** *= deathlike*

Exceptions: words that end with the letters **ch** or **sh** behave in a different way for noun plurals and for the third personal singular form, in that you add **es**, for example:

bunch + **es** *= bunches*
push + **es** *= pushes*

Exceptions: if a word ends with **ch** and it is pronounced like the letter **k**, rather than the 'tch' sound at the end of **coach**, **lunch** and **witch**, you add **s** to make it plural, for example:

matriarch + **s** *= matriarchs*
monarch + **s** *= monarchs*
stomach + **s** *= stomachs*

Exceptions: there are a few Scottish words ending with **ch** that are used in standard British English, for example **loch** and **Sassenach**. In the Scottish accent this letter combination within Scots words is pronounced with a soft noise at the back of the throat, while many non-Scots pronounce it as **k**. A widely quoted phrase that illustrates this sound in Scots is 'a braw bricht moonlicht nicht'. Scots nouns that end with **ch** become plural by adding **s**, rather than **es**, for example:

loch + **s** *= lochs*
pibroch + **s** *= pibrochs*
quaich + **s** *= quaichs*
Sassenach + **s** *= Sassenachs*

WORDS THAT END WITH THE LETTER l

- *plural noun – add* **s**: *bikini +* **s** *= bikinis*
- *third person singular – add* **s**: *ski +* **s** *= skis*

- *present participle – add* **ing**: *ski* + **ing** = *skiing*
- *past tense – add* **ed**: *ski* + **ed** = *skied*
- *derived form – add* **suffix**: *ski* + **er** = *skier*

WORDS THAT END WITH THE LETTER J

Plural noun – add **es**: raj + **es** = rajes; hadj + **es** = hadjes

> ## Insight
> Very few words in English end with the letter **j**. **Raj** is a Hindi word meaning 'government' and is used mainly to refer to the former British rule of India. **Hadj** (and its variants **haj** and **hajj**) is Arabic for 'effort'. The **hadj** is the annual pilgrimage made by Muslims to Mecca.

WORDS THAT END WITH THE LETTER K

- *plural noun – add* **s**: *beak* + **s** = *beaks*
- *comparative – add* **er**: *black* + **er** = *blacker*
- *superlative – add* **est**: *weak* + **est** = *weakest*
- *third person singular – add* **s**: *thank* + **s** = *thanks*
- *present participle – add* **ing**: *stink* + **ing** = *stinking*
- *past tense – add* **ed**: *talk* + **ed** = *talked*
- *derived form – add* **suffix**: *duck* + **ling** = *duckling*

WORDS THAT END WITH THE LETTER L

- *plural noun – add* **s**: *doll* + **s** = *dolls*
- *comparative – add* **er**: *tall* + **er** = *taller*
- *superlative – add* **est**: *full* + **est** = *fullest*
- *third person singular – add* **s**: *label* + **s** = *labels*
- *present participle – add* **ing**: *steal* + **ing** = *stealing*
- *past tense – add* **ed**: *cool* + **ed** = *cooled*
- *derived form – add* **suffix**: *spill* + **age** = *spillage*;
  girl + **hood** = *girlhood*

Exceptions: the following adjectives double the final **l** before adding **er** or **est**:

cruel → *cruell* + **er** = *crueller; cruell* + **est** = *cruellest*
evil → *evill* + **er** = *eviller; evill* + **est** = *evillest*

Exceptions: if a verb ends with a single vowel followed by a single letter l, you double the l before adding **ing** or **ed**; if a word ends with a single vowel followed by a single letter l, you double the l before adding a suffix that begins with a vowel or the letter **y**:

cancel → *cancell* + **ing** = *cancelling*
joyful → *joyfull* + **y** = *joyfully*
label → *labell* + **ed** = *labelled*
control → *controll* + **able** = *controllable*
marvel → *marvell* + **ous** = *marvellous*
pal → *pall* + **y** = *pally*

Exceptions: the following verbs also double the final l before adding **ing**, **ed** or a suffix that begins with a vowel:

dial → *diall* + **ing** = *dialling; diall* + **ed** = *dialled*
duel → *duell* + **ing** = *duelling; duell* + **ed** = *duelled*
fuel → *fuell* + **ing** = *fuelling; fuell* + **ed** = *fuelled*
dial → *diall* + **er** = *dialler*
duel → *duell* + **ist** = *duellist*
fuel → *fuell* + **er** = *fueller*

Note that when you add the suffix **y** to the adjective **wool**, you double the final l:

wool → *wooll* + **y** = *woolly*

There is also a small group of two-syllable nouns ending with a single vowel followed by letter l that obeys this rule and doubles the final l before adding the suffix **y**:

gravel → *gravell* + **y** = *gravelly*
weasel → *weasell* + **y** = *weaselly*

WORDS THAT END WITH THE LETTER M

▶ *plural noun – add* s: *organism* + s = *organisms*
▶ *comparative – add* er: *warm* + er = *warmer*
▶ *superlative – add* est: *calm* + est = *calmest*
▶ *third person singular – add* s: *dream* + s = *dreams*
▶ *present participle – add* ing: *farm* + ing = *farming*
▶ *past tense – add* ed: *steam* + ed = *steamed*
▶ *derived form – add* suffix: *perform* + ance = *performance*

Exceptions: for some adjectives and verbs that end in an **m**, you double the **m** before adding **er, est, ing** and **ed**. These are adjectives and verbs of one syllable that end with a single vowel followed by **m**; and also verbs of more than one syllable that end with a single short vowel followed by **m**, in which the stress is on the end of the word. If a one-syllable word ends with a short vowel followed by an **m**, you double the **m** before adding a suffix beginning with a vowel or the letter **y**:

grim → *grimm* + er = *grimmer*
glum → *glumm* + est = *glummest*
jam → *jamm* + ing = *jamming*
stem → *stemm* + ed = *stemmed*
retrim → *retrimm* + ing = *retrimming*
retrim → *retrimm* + ed = *retrimmed*
drum → *drumm* + er = *drummer*
scum → *scumm* + y = *scummy*

WORDS THAT END WITH THE LETTER N

▶ *plural noun – add* s: *baboon* + s = *baboons*
▶ *comparative – add* er: *mean* + er = *meaner*
▶ *superlative – add* est: *common* + est = *commonest*
▶ *third person singular – add* s: *run* + s = *runs*
▶ *present participle – add* ing: *listen* + ing = *listening*
▶ *past tense – add* ed: *moan* + ed = *moaned*
▶ *derived form – add* suffix: *contain* + ment = *containment*

Exceptions: for some adjectives and verbs that end in an **n**, you double the **n** before adding **er, est, ing** and **ed**. These are adjectives and verbs of one syllable that end with a single vowel followed by **n**; and also verbs of more than one syllable that end with a single short vowel followed by **n**, in which the stress is on the end of the word. If a one-syllable word ends with a short vowel followed by an **n**, you double the **n** before adding a suffix beginning with a vowel or the letter **y**; if a word has more than one syllable and ends with a single short vowel followed by **n** and the stress is on the end of the word, then you double the **n** before adding a suffix beginning with a vowel or letter **y**:

thin → *thinn* + **er** = *thinner*
wan → *wann* + **est** = *wannest*
run → *runn* + **ing** = *running*
ban → *bann* + **ed** = *banned*
begin → *beginn* + **ing** = *beginning*
japan → *japann* + **ed** = *japanned*
win → *winn* + **able** = *winnable*
begin → *beginn* + **er** = *beginner*

WORDS THAT END WITH THE LETTER O

▶ *plural noun – see below*
▶ *third person singular – add* **s**: *tattoo* + **s** = *tattoos*
▶ *present participle – add* **ing**: *tattoo* + **ing** = *tattooing*
▶ *past tense – add* **ed**: *tattoo* + **ed** = *tattooed*
▶ *derived form – add* **suffix**: *two* + **some** = *twosome*

Plural noun: for most nouns ending with **o**, you add **s** to make the plural, for example:

cameo + **s** = *cameos*

However, there are a few nouns ending in **o** that add **es** to make them plural. These are:

bubo + **es** = *buboes*
buffalo + **es** = *buffaloes*

cargo + **es** = *cargoes*
dingo + **es** = *dingoes*
echo + **es** = *echoes*
embargo + **es** = *embargoes*
hero + **es** = *heroes*
lingo + **es** = *lingoes*
potato + **es** = *potatoes*
tomato + **es** = *tomatoes*
veto + **es** = *vetoes*
volcano + **es** = *volcanoes*

There are also a number of nouns ending with **o** that can become plural by adding either **s** *or* **es**. Some of these are listed below, with the most common plural first:

domino → *dominoes* or *dominos*
grotto → *grottoes* or *grottos*
mango → *mangoes* or *mangos*
memento → *mementoes* or *mementos*
motto → *mottoes* or *mottos*
mosquito → *mosquitoes* or *mosquitos*
torpedo → *torpedoes* or *torpedos*
banjo → *banjos* or *banjoes*
dodo → *dodos* or *dodoes*
flamingo → *flamingos* or *flamingoes*
ghetto → *ghettos* or *ghettoes*
halo → *halos* or *haloes*

WORDS THAT END WITH THE LETTER P

▶ *plural noun – add* **s**: *wasp* + **s** = *wasps*
▶ *comparative – add* **er**: *plump* + **er** = *plumper*
▶ *superlative – add* **est**: *deep* + **est** = *deepest*
▶ *third person singular – add* **s**: *limp* + **s** = *limps*
▶ *present participle – add* **ing**: *scoop* + **ing** = *scooping*
▶ *past tense – add* **ed**: *grasp* + **ed** = *grasped*
▶ *derived form – add* **suffix**: *help* + **ful** = *helpful*

Exceptions: if an adjective with one syllable ends with a single vowel followed by the letter **p**, you double the **p** before adding **er** or **est**, for example:

hip → *hipp* + **er** = *hipper*
crap → *crapp* + **est** = *crappest*

Exceptions: if a verb ends with a single vowel followed by **p**, you double the **p** before adding **ing** or **ed**, for example:

trip → *tripp* + **ing** = *tripping*
kidnap → *kidnapp* + **ed** = *kidnapped*

Exceptions: the exceptions to the previous rule (the verbs that end with a single vowel followed by a letter **p** that do *not* double the **p** before adding **ing** or **ed**) are:

develop + **ing** = *developing; develop* + **ed** = *developed*
gossip + **ing** = *gossiping; gossip* + **ed** = *gossiped*
gallop + **ing** = *galloping; gallop* + **ed** = *galloped*
wallop + **ing** = *walloping; wallop* + **ed** = *walloped*
hiccup + **ing** = *hiccuping; hiccup* + **ed** = *hiccupped*

Exceptions: if a word ends with a single vowel followed by **p**, you double the **p** before adding a suffix that begins with a vowel, for example:

ship → *shipp* + **able** = *shippable*
eavesdrop → *eavesdropp* + **er** = *eavesdropper*

Exceptions: the exceptions to the previous rule (the words that that end with a single vowel followed by a letter **p** that do *not* double the **p** before adding a suffix that begins with a vowel) are:

develop + **er** = *developer*
gallop + **er** = *galloper*

WORDS THAT END WITH THE LETTER R

▶ *plural noun – add* **s**: *colour* + **s** = *colours*
▶ *comparative – add* **er**: *clear* + **er** = *clearer*
▶ *superlative – add* **est**: *dear* + **est** = *dearest*
▶ *third person singular – add* **s**: *confer* + **s** = *confers*
▶ *present participle – add* **ing**: *fear* + **ing** = *fearing*
▶ *past tense – add* **ed**: *jeer* + **ed** = *jeered*
▶ *derived form – add* **suffix**: *deliver* + **y** = *delivery*; *beer* + **y** = *beery*

Exceptions: for some verbs that end in an **r**, you double the **r** before adding **ing** and **ed**. These are verbs of one syllable that end with a single vowel followed by **r** and also verbs of more than one syllable that end with a single short vowel followed by **r**, in which the stress is on the end of the word. If a one-syllable word ends with a short vowel followed by an **r**, you double the **r** before adding a suffix that begins with a vowel or the letter **y**. If a word has more than one syllable and ends with a single short vowel followed by **r** and the stress is on the end of the word, then you double the **r** before adding a suffix beginning with a vowel or **y**:

bar → *barr* + **ing** = *barring*
whir → *whirr* + **ed** = *whirred*
recur → *recurr* + **ing** = *recurring*
abhor → *abhorr* + **ed** = *abhorred*
fur → *furr* + **y** = *furry*
occur → *occurr* + **ence** = *occurrence*

Adding a suffix to a word that ends with our
Certain suffixes that begin with a vowel have an effect on words that end with the letters **our**. These suffixes are **ous**, **ary**, **ious**, **ize**, **ific**, **iferous**, **ist** and **al**. When you add one of these suffixes to a word that ends with **our**, you have to drop the letter **u** before the **r**, for example:

rigour → *rigor* + **ous** = *rigorous*
clamour → *clamor* + **ous** = *clamorous*
honour → *honor* + **ary** = *honorary*

labour → *labor* + **ious** = *laborious*
glamour → *glamor* + **ize** = *glamorize*
humour → *humor* + **ist** = *humorist*

WORDS THAT END WITH THE LETTER S

▶ *plural noun* – *add* **es**: *bus* + **es** = *buses*
▶ *comparative* – *add* **er**: *cross* + **er** = *crosser*
▶ *superlative* – *add* **est**: *cross* + **est** = *crossest*
▶ *third person singular* – *add* **es**: *miss* + **es** = *misses*
▶ *present participle* – *add* **ing**: *kiss* + **ing** = *kissing*
▶ *past tense* – *add* **ed**: *fuss* + **ed** = *fussed*
▶ *derived form* – *add* **suffix**: *access* + **ible** = *accessible*

Verbs that end with a single **s** are unusual in English and, perhaps for this reason, there is often rather a lot of confusion around them. Some add **ing** and **ed** without doubling the **s**, some double the **s** and then add **ing** and **ed**, and some can do either:

chorus + **ing** = *chorusing*; *chorus* + **ed** = *chorused*
nonplus → *nonpluss* + **ing** = *nonplussing*; *nonpluss* + **ed** = *nonplussed*
bus → *bussing* or *busing*; *bussed* or *bused*
gas → *gassing* or *gasing*; *gassed* or *gased*
bias → *biasing* or *biassing*; *biased* or *biassed*
focus → *focusing* or *focussing*; *focused* or *focussed*

Insight

Interestingly, for the one-syllable verbs **bus** and **gas**, the double **s** version is commoner than the single **s** version, while the reverse is true for the two-syllable words **bias** and **focus**. This may be due to the influence of other one-syllable words that end with a vowel and then a consonant, such as **cut** and **map**.

Exceptions: when you add the suffix **y** to a one-syllable word ending with a single **s**, you must double the **s** first:

gas → *gass* + **y** = *gassy*

WORDS THAT END WITH THE LETTER T

▶ *plural noun – add* s: *cat* + s = *cats*
▶ *comparative – add* er: *short* + er = *shorter*
▶ *superlative – add* est: *quaint* + est = *quaintest*
▶ *third person singular – add* s: *eat* + s = *eats*
▶ *present participle – add* ing: *hurt* + ing = *hurting*
▶ *past tense – add* ed: *visit* + ed = *visited*
▶ *derived form – add* suffix: *bucket* + ful = *bucketful*

Exceptions: for some adjectives and verbs that end in a t, you double the t before adding er, est, ing and ed. These are adjectives and verbs of one syllable that end with a single vowel followed by t and also verbs of more than one syllable that end with a single short vowel followed by t, in which the stress is on the end of the word. If a one-syllable word ends with a short vowel followed by a t, you double the t before adding a suffix that begins with a vowel or letter y. If a word has more than one syllable and ends with a single short vowel followed by a t and the stress is on the end of the word, then you double the t before adding a suffix beginning with a vowel or letter y:

fat → *fatt* + er = *fatter*
wet → *wett* + est = *wettest*
set → *sett* + ing = *setting*
fit → *fitt* + ed = *fitted*
admit → *admitt* + ing = *admitting*
abet → *abett* + ed = *abetted*
hit → *hitt* + able = *hittable*
acquit → *acquitt* + al = *acquittal*

WORDS THAT END WITH THE LETTER U

▶ *plural noun – add* s: *emu* + s = *emus*
▶ *third person singular – add* s: *plateau* + s = *plateaus*
▶ *present participle – add* ing: *plateau* + ing = *plateauing*
▶ *past tense – add* ed: *plateau* + ed = *plateaued*

Exceptions: nouns that end with eau. If a noun ends with the letters eau, you have a choice of either adding x or s. This is because words that end in eau have come into the English language from French.

In French the plural of this kind of word is made by adding **x**, while in English you add **s**. You can use either ending now in English, as long as you stick to one style within a piece of writing.

gateau → *gateau*x or *gateau*s
plateau → *plateau*x or *plateau*s
trousseau → *trousseau*x or *trousseau*s

WORDS THAT END WITH THE LETTER V

▶ *plural noun – add* **s**: *Slav* + **s** = *Slavs*
▶ *third person singular – add* **s**: *rev* + **s** = *revs*
▶ *present participle – double* **v** *and add* **ing**: *rev* → *revv* + **ing** = *revving*
▶ *past tense – double* **v** *and add* **ed**: *rev* → *revv* + **ed** = *revved*
▶ *derived form – add* **suffix**: *chav* + **like** = *chavlike*

Exceptions: if you add the y suffix to a word ending with **v**, you have to double the **v** first, for example:

chav → *chavv* + **y** = *chavvy*

WORDS THAT END WITH THE LETTER W

▶ *plural noun – add* **s**: *rainbow* + **s** = *rainbows*
▶ *comparative – add* **er**: *yellow* + **er** = *yellower*
▶ *superlative – add* **est**: *narrow* + **est** = *narrowest*
▶ *third person singular – add* **s**: *flow* + **s** = *flows*
▶ *present participle – add* **ing**: *chew* + **ing** = *chewing*
▶ *past tense – add* **ed**: *follow* + **ed** = *followed*
▶ *derived form – add* **suffix**: *widow* + **hood** = *widowhood*

WORDS THAT END WITH THE LETTER X

▶ *plural noun – add* **es**: *hoax* + **es** = *hoaxes*
▶ *third person singular – add* **es**: *flummox* + **es** = *flummoxes*
▶ *present participle – add* **ing**: *box* + **ing** = *boxing*
▶ *past tense – add* **ed**: *coax* + **ed** = *coaxed*
▶ *derived form – add* **suffix**: *sex* + **y** = *sexy*

WORDS THAT END WITH THE LETTER Y

How we treat words that end with a y when we add a suffix often depends on the letter that comes before the y.

► *plural noun – if a noun ends with the letters* **ay, ey, oy** *or* **uy,** *the plural is made by adding* **s,** *for example:*
tray + **s** = *trays*
key + **s** = *keys*
alloy + **s** = *alloys*
guy + **s** = *guys*

► *if a noun ends with a consonant followed by* **y,** *you change the* **y** *to* **i** *and then add* **es,** *for example:*
ruby → *rubi* + **es** = *rubies*
trophy → *trophi* + **es** = *trophies*
party → *parti* + **es** = *parties*

Exception: a noun that ends with the letters **quy** follows the style of **ruby, trophy** and **party,** for example:

soliloquy → *soliloqui* + **es** = *soliloquies*

► *comparative and superlative – if an adjective ends with the letters* **ay, ey** *or* **oy,** *you add* **er** *and* **est,** *for example:*
gay + **er** = *gayest*
fey + **er** = *feyer*
coy + **est** = *coyest*

► *when the final* **y** *is preceded by any letter other than* **a, e** *or* **o,** *you change the* **y** *to* **i** *and add either* **er** *or* **est,** *for example:*
flabby → *flabbi* + **er** = *flabbier*
wealthy → *wealthi* + **er** = *wealthier*
lucky → *lucki* + **est** = *luckiest*
heavy → *heavi* + **est** = *heaviest*

Exception: there is a small group of adjectives ending in y that can be treated in two ways. These are **dry, shy, sly, spry** and **wry.** You can change the y to i before adding **er** or **est,** but you can also keep the y as it is before adding the ending. For all these words both forms are correct but one form tends to be much more common than the other (the most common form is shown first below):

dry → *drier* or *dryer; driest* or *dryest*
shy → *shyer* or *shier; shyest* or *shiest*
sly → *slyer* or *slier; slyest* or *sliest*
spry → *spryer* or *sprier; spryest* or *spriest*
wry → *wryer* or *wrier; wryest* or *wriest*

The spelling **dryer** is the one commonly used for the noun, as in *hairdryer* and *tumble dryer*.

▶ *third person singular – if a verb ends with the letters* **ay, ey, oy** *or* **uy,** *you add* **s,** *for example:*
  stay + **s** = *stays*
  convey + **s** = *conveys*
  annoy + **s** = *annoys*
  buy + **s** = *buys*
▶ *if any other letter comes before the* **y,** *you change the* **y** *to* **i** *and add* **es,** *for example:*
  lobby → *lobbi* + **es** = *lobbies*
  apply → *appli* + **es** = *applies*
  copy → *copi* + **es** = *copies*

▶ *present participle – add* **ing:** *delay* + **ing** = *delaying;*
  clarify + **ing** = *clarifying*
▶ *past tense – if the verb ends with the letters* **ay, ey, oy** *or* **uy,** *you add* **ed,** *for example: convey* + **ed** = *conveyed; destroy* + **ed** = *destroyed*

Exceptions: the verbs **lay, say** and **pay** have an irregular past tense:

lay → *laid*
say → *said*
pay → *paid*

- if the letter before the **y** is a consonant, you change the **y** to **i** and then add **ed**, for example:
  *ready → readi + **ed** = readied*
  *deny → deni + **ed** = denied*
  *envy → envi + **ed** = envied*

- *adding suffixes – if the word ends with* **ay, ey, oy** *or* **uy***, add the suffix to the word as it is, for example:*
  *pay + **ment** = payment*
  *grey + **ness** = greyness*
- *if the* **y** *is preceded by a consonant, change the* **y** *to* **i** *before adding the suffix, for example:*
  *rely → reli + **able** = reliable*
  *happy → happi + **ness** = happiness*
  *likely → likeli + **hood** = likelihood*

Exceptions: for the adjectives **shy, sly, spry** and **wry** you do not change the **y** to **i** before adding a suffix:

shy → shyly; shyness
sly → slyly; slyness
spry → spryly; spryness
wry → wryly; wryness

Things are not so clear-cut for the adjective **dry**, however. When you add **able** or **ness**, you keep the **y**, so:

dry → dryable; dryness

But when you add **ly** to create an adverb, you can either change the **y** to **i** or leave it as it is, so:

dry → drily or dryly

Both adverbs are correct but **drily** occurs much more frequently than **dryly**.

When you add **er** to **dry** to make the noun that means 'a thing or person that dries', once again you have the choice of changing the **y** to **i**, or leaving it as it is. In this case the form **dryer** is much commoner than **drier**:

dry → dryer or drier

This is for the noun from **dry**. The comparative adjective is usually spelt with **i**, so:

*The sheets will be **drier** if you put them in the tumble **dryer**.*

WORDS THAT END WITH THE LETTER Z

▶ *plural noun – add* **s**: *topaz +* **es** *= topazes*
▶ *third person singular – add* **es**: *buzz +* **es** *= buzzes*
▶ *present participle – add* **ing**: *waltz +* **ing** *= waltzing*
▶ *past tense – add* **ed**: *blitz +* **ed** *= blitzed*
▶ *derived form – add* **suffix**: *fuzz +* **y** *= fuzzy*

Exceptions: if the word is a one-syllable noun or verb that ends with a vowel followed by a single **z**, you double the **z** before adding the noun plural ending **es** or the verb ending **es**, **ing** or **ed**, for example:

fez → fezz + **es** *= fezzes*
quiz → quizz + **es** *= quizzes*
quiz → quizz + **ing** *= quizzing*
whiz → whizz + **ed** *= whizzed*

Some other unusual noun plurals

English is the magpie of languages. No other language has adopted and adapted so many words from so many different sources. (You can learn more about this in Chapter 11). Because of this, there are groups of nouns within English that follow the rules of other languages when they become plural, most notably the rules of Latin and Greek.

SOME NOUNS THAT END WITH THE LETTERS ON

English has a number of Greek words that end with the letters **on**, and the plurals of these words are made by replacing the **on** with **a**, for example:

criterion → *criteria*
phenomenon → *phenomena*
automaton → *automata*

SOME NOUNS THAT END WITH THE LETTERS UM

There are a number of Latin nouns ending in **um** which retain the Latin plural form. In this, the **um** is changed to **a**, for example:

addendum → *addenda*
bacterium → *bacteria*
ovum → *ova*
podium → *podia*
spectrum → *spectra*

Some Latin nouns that end in **um** can have two plural forms: with the Latin ending **a**, or the English ending **s**. This happens with many words that come into English from other languages. They start off with their own native plural form, and then, as the words become naturalized and established in English, they adopt the commonest English noun plural ending – the letter **s** – and both plurals are used. Some examples of these are:

aquarium → *aquariums* or *aquaria*
cerebellum → *cerebella* or *cerebellums*
crematorium → *crematoria* or *crematoriums*
curriculum → *curricula* or *curriculums*
gymnasium → *gymnasiums* or *gymnasia*
memorandum → *memoranda* or *memorandums*
millennium → *millennia* or *millenniums*
plectrum → *plectrums* or *plectra*

referendum → *referendums* or *referenda*
stadium → *stadiums* or *stadia*

A general point to notice about this is that the more technical or unusual the word, the likelier it is for the Latin plural to be used, for example **cerebellum** and **curriculum**. The commoner a word is in English, the greater the likelihood of it becoming naturalized so that its plural is Anglicized too, for example **aquarium, gymnasium, plectrum** and **referendum**.

It is actually possible to see this happening over a period of time. In 1990 *The Taylor Report* was published in Britain. This was a study into the safety of sports grounds that had been commissioned by the government in response to the Hillsborough Disaster, in which over 90 fans of Liverpool Football Club were crushed to death at the start of a cup match at the home stadium of Sheffield Wednesday. The purpose of this report was to investigate the reasons for the disaster and to make recommendations for ensuring safety at sporting events in the future. One of the key aspects of the report was a review of the safety of football **stadiums** – or is it football **stadia**? Lord Taylor used the Latin plural **stadia** over 40 times, but never the Anglicized form **stadiums**. This is not that surprising, given that it is an official document, commissioned by the government, and written by a high court judge. This type of writing will always tend towards formal language and the Latin plural is an indication of this.

Now, 20 years later, when I compare the hits for **stadiums** and **stadia** in the search engine Google, these are the figures I find: about 6,900,000 for **stadiums** and about 1,830,000 for **stadia**. The English plural **stadiums** outnumbers the Latin plural **stadia** by more than three to one.

You could argue that this is because the internet is unedited and unchecked and therefore contains many thousands of spelling mistakes, and the fact that one form is preferred over another proves nothing. However, the huge difference in the number of occurrences is significant. Even words that are often misspelt usually have more hits for the correct spelling on the internet. For example, while **accomodate** (the common misspelling with only one **m**) has an impressive number of occurrences (about 3,750,000), the correct spelling **accommodate** still has a whopping 36 million hits, almost 10 times as many as its misspelt form.

The example of **stadiums** and **stadia** is not about right and wrong spelling, of course, but about the tendency of English to absorb foreign words and then make them behave more like English words. Both **stadiums** and **stadia** are correct plurals for **stadium**, but **stadiums** is gradually asserting itself as the dominant form. We see this reinforced when we look at some of the online occurrences of **stadiums**, which include *The Independent* ('Giving the name away: Stadiums named after sponsors'), The BBC ('Workers building stadiums for next year's World Cup are ending a week-long strike') and *The Times* ('The top ten football stadiums').

SOME NOUNS THAT END WITH THE LETTERS US

A group of English words that come from Latin end with the letters **us**. Their plural is formed by replacing **us** with the letter **i**, for example:

alumnus → *alumni*
bacillus → *bacilli*
nucleus → *nuclei*
stimulus → *stimuli*

As with the nouns that end in **um**, some words that end with **us** can also have an Anglicized plural form (by adding **es**), for example:

abacus → *abaci* or *abacuses*
cactus → *cacti* or *cactuses*
focus → *foci* or *focuses*
fungus → *fungi* or *funguses*
hippopotamus → *hippopotamuses* or *hippopotami*
radius → *radii* or *radiuses*

syllabus → *syllabi* or *syllabuses*
terminus → *termini* or *terminuses*
thesaurus → *thesauruses* or *thesauri*
uterus → *uteri* or *uteruses*

When you do an internet search for the two plural forms of the nouns above, in all but two cases the Latin plural is far commoner than the Anglicized form. The first exception is **hippopotamus.** There are about the same number of occurrences of both, with **hippopotamuses** slightly outnumbering **hippopotami.** Both plurals are clumsy but the Latin form does also sound rather ridiculous, which may explain the slight preference for **hippopotamuses.**

Insight

The noun **thesaurus** has two possible plurals: **thesauruses** and **thesauri.** A search on Google shows that **thesauruses** is four times as popular as **thesauri.** And yet bookshops tend to label their shelves 'Dictionaries and Thesauri'. I suspect this is connected with a fear of appearing ignorant of the 'proper' (that is, the Latin) plural. In over 20 years I have never heard anyone who works in dictionary publishing say anything other than **thesauruses** as the plural of **thesaurus.**

SOME NOUNS THAT END WITH THE LETTER A

A number of English words from Latin end with the letter **a.** The plural is made by adding **e,** for example:

alumna → *alumnae*
larva → *larvae*
vertebra → *vertebrae*

Some of these nouns can also have the English **s** plural form, for example:

antenna → *antennae* or *antennas*
formula → *formulae* or *formulas*
supernova → *supernovae* or *supernovas*

The plural is **antennae** when **antenna** means 'an insect's feeler' and **antennas** when it means 'a television aerial'.

English also has a group of Greek nouns ending in **a**. The Greek plural is made by adding **ta** to the end of the word, but these words also have Anglicized plurals made by adding **s**, for example:

carcinoma → *carcinomas* or *carcinomata*
lymphoma → *lymphomas* or *lymphomata*
sarcoma → *sarcomas* or *sarcomata*
schema → *schemas* or *schemata*
stigma → *stigmata* or *stigmas*
stoma → *stomata* or *stomas*
trauma → *traumas* or *traumata*

For most of these words the Anglicized plural is more commonly found than the Greek plural.

When **stigma** is used to mean 'a flower part' or 'a mark of disgrace', the plural is **stigmas**. When it means 'a mark on the body that is similar to the marks of crucifixion on the body of Christ', the plural is **stigmata**. It usually occurs in the plural form of **stigmata** rather than the singular.

If **stoma** means 'a pore on a plant' or 'an opening in the surface of a living thing', the plural is **stomata**. When **stoma** is used to refer to an opening created in the body through which waste can be passed, the plural is usually **stomas**.

SOME NOUNS THAT END WITH THE LETTERS EX

Some Latin nouns in English end with the letters **ex** and these can have either of two plurals. You can either replace **ex** with **ices**, or you can add **es** to the end of the word, for example:

ibex → *ibexes* or *ibices*
index → *indices* or *indexes*
vertex → *vertices* or *vertexes*
vortex → *vortices* or *vortexes*

When **index** means 'a list of things in a book' the plural is **indexes** and when it means 'a pointer' or 'a mathematical symbol' the plural is **indices**.

SOME NOUNS THAT END WITH THE LETTERS IX

Some Latin nouns in English end with the letters **ix** and these can have either of two plurals. You can either replace **ix** with **ices**, or you can add **es** to the end of the word, for example:

appendix → *appendices* or *appendixes*
cervix → *cervixes* or *cervices*
dominatrix → *dominatrices* or *dominatrixes*
executrix → *executrices* or *executrixes*
helix → *helices* or *helixes*
matrix → *matrices* or *matrixes*

When an **appendix** is a part added to a book or document, the plural is **appendices**. When an **appendix** is the part of the body that is often removed, the plural is **appendixes**.

SOME NOUNS THAT END WITH THE LETTERS NX

English has a small group of Greek nouns that end with the letters **nx**. To make the plural you can either change the **x** to **g** and add **es**, or add **es** to the end of the word, for example:

larynx → *larynxes* or *larynges*
phalanx → *phalanges* or *phalanxes*
pharynx → *pharynges* or *pharynxes*
sphinx → *sphinxes* or *sphinges*

When **phalanx** means 'a bone in the finger or toe', the plural is **phalanges**. When **phalanx** means 'a formation of soldiers' or 'a group of supporters', the plural is **phalanxes**.

It is interesting to note that, of these four words, those with the most occurrences in Google are **larynx** (with almost seven million hits) and **sphinx** (with over seven and a half million hits). The next most frequent word is **phalanx**, with a mere two million occurrences. For both **larynx** and **sphinx**, the **es** plural is commoner than the **ges** form. Once again we can see that the more often a foreign word is used in English, the more likely it is for the Anglicized plural to be preferred over the original.

SOME NOUNS THAT END WITH THE LETTERS IS

There are a number of English nouns ending with the letters **is** that come from Greek. The plural of these words is formed by replacing **is** at the end with **es**, for example:

analysis → *analyses*
axis → *axes*
basis → *bases*
crisis → *crises*
ellipsis → *ellipses*
genesis → *geneses*
oasis → *oases*
synthesis → *syntheses*
thesis → *theses*

Insight

These words change their pronunciation when they become plural. The final syllable changes from 'is' to 'eez', so while **thesis** is pronounced '**thee-sis**', its plural **theses** is pronounced '**thee-seez**'.

Exercise

The following sentences show a noun or nouns in bold. Can you make these singular nouns plural? You will have to remove some words like **a**, **an** and **the**, and change others like **his** to **their**.

1 I like to take a **bunch** of grapes when I visit my **uncle** in hospital.
2 The **berry** had frozen on the **branch** of the holly **bush** in our **garden**.
3 He had put **shampoo**, **soap**, a face **cloth** and **aftershave** on the **shelf** in the bathroom.

4 The **bailiff** and his **wife** brought us a tea **caddy** and an **avocado**.
5 Did you get the **memo** I sent about the windows for the new **embassy**?
6 Please leave your **scarf**, **glove** and **umbrella** in the hall.
7 Lynne is studying the **phenomenon** of the missing **giraffe**.
8 That **company** is famous for treating its **staff** appallingly.
9 No **zoo** in this country has a **cheetah**, a **rhino**, an **emu**, a **zebra**, a **baboon** and a **chimpanzee** living in the same **enclosure**.
10 The **biography** of a famous war **hero** forms the **basis** for the **film**.

Exercise

Take the following adjectives and change them into:
a their comparative form (that's the one that means 'more') and then
b their superlative form (that's the one that means 'the most').

▶ *black*
▶ *yummy*
▶ *red*
▶ *limp*
▶ *dreary*
▶ *twee*
▶ *fey*
▶ *fierce*
▶ *hip*
▶ *severe*

Exercise

Make the third person singular present tense form of each of the following verbs by adding either **es** or **s** first. You may need to make a change to the end of the verb first.

▶ *pray*
▶ *defend*
▶ *shampoo*

(Contd)

- ▶ *blitz*
- ▶ *carry*
- ▶ *shanghai*
- ▶ *fuss*
- ▶ *laugh*
- ▶ *coach*
- ▶ *fix*

Exercise

Make the present participle of each of the following verbs by adding **ing**. You may need to make a change to the end of the verb first.

- ▶ *dub*
- ▶ *feel*
- ▶ *note*
- ▶ *propel*
- ▶ *skip*
- ▶ *knee*
- ▶ *gas*
- ▶ *frolic*
- ▶ *mar*
- ▶ *boogie*

Exercise

Make the past tense of the each of the following verbs by adding **ed** or **d**. You may need to make a change to the end of the verb first.

- ▶ *contrive*
- ▶ *plod*
- ▶ *conceal*
- ▶ *swoop*
- ▶ *appal*
- ▶ *top*
- ▶ *frolic*

- *bus*
- *poke*
- *party*

Add the suffix to the end of the word in each of the following pairs. Remember that you might need to change the word first.

- *white + ness*
- *merry + ment*
- *guitar + ist*
- *council + or*
- *snake + y*
- *gentle + ness*
- *knowledge + able*
- *capable + y*
- *trespass + er*
- *classify + able*
- *frolic + y*
- *namedrop + er*
- *grieve + ance*
- *humour + ous*
- *fad + y*
- *pretty + ly*
- *wreck + age*
- *help + less*
- *develop + er*
- *appreciate + ive*

'i before e except after c'

The rule 'i before e except after c' is one that most people remember from school days, even if the rest of what they learnt about spelling is rather hazy. The rule needs a little more explanation. The letter i and the letter e can combine to make the sound 'ee' (that is the vowel sound in **feel**), and this is where the 'i before e except after c' rule applies. For most words that contain this letter sound, the i comes before the e, for example:

achieve	*grieve*	*shield*
belief	*hygiene*	*siege*
believe	*niece*	*thief*
brief	*piece*	*thieve*
chief	*pierce*	*wield*
field	*relief*	*yield*
fierce	*relieve*	
grief	*retrieve*	

Exceptions: there is a small group of words with the vowel sound 'ee' in which the e comes before the i, even though e is not coming after letter c, for example:

caffeine
codeine
Keith
protein
seize
Sheila
weir
weird

Apparent exceptions: there are another three words that appear to be exceptions to the rule: **either**, **neither** and **heinous**. The vowel sound in the first syllable of each of these words can be pronounced as 'ee' which, strictly speaking, makes these exceptions to the rule. However, for each of these words the pronunciation with the 'ee' vowel sound occurs far less frequently than another pronunciation, 'eye' for **either** and **neither** and 'ay' for **heinous**. So, when these pronunciations are used, **either**, **neither** and **heinous** do not break the rule about 'i before e except after c' when they make the sound 'ee'.

When e and i combine to make the sound 'ee' and they follow the letter c, the e comes first, for example:

ceiling
conceit
conceive
deceit
deceive
perceive
receipt
receive

Exceptions: the second syllables of **species** and **specie** (money in the form of coins) both have the 'ee' sound, but the **i** comes before the **e**, even though it is after **c**.

Exercise

Insert either **ei** or **ie** into the following words in order to complete them:

▶ f**ld *(place where cows graze)*
▶ s**ze *(take by force)*
▶ gr**f *(great unhappiness)*
▶ sh**la *(informal Australian word for a woman)*
▶ th**f *(someone who steals)*
▶ prot**n *(compound found in chicken)*
▶ caff**ne *(chemical found in coffee)*
▶ sh**ld *(protective object)*
▶ br**f *(short)*
▶ w**rd *(strange or bizarre)*
▶ p**rce *(poke a hole in)*
▶ spec**s *(classification of a living thing)*
▶ hyg**ne *(cleanliness)*
▶ h**nous *(evil)*
▶ c**ling *(top part of a room)*
▶ ach**ve *(manage to do)*
▶ f**rce *(very dangerous or angry)*
▶ rec**pt *(piece of paper proving you've bought something)*
▶ **ther *(one or the other)*
▶ n**ce *(daughter of your brother or sister)*

ize versus ise

Many British people were taught at school that a certain group of verbs should always end with **ise** and that to use **ize** is to debase the language of Shakespeare with a ghastly Americanism. This is a view popularly held to this day. However popular it may be though, the idea that **ise** is British and **ize** is American is quite wrong. Both spelling forms have been recognized in English for centuries and, indeed, the *Oxford English Dictionary* prefers the **ize** spellings, pointing out that the suffix **ise** is a 'variant spelling of IZE', confirming **ize** as the standard. The preference for **ize** was partly due to its closeness to the Greek verb ending **izo**. American English has preferred the **ize** form as its standard for over a century, and this has led to the mistaken belief that this spelling is purely an American one, and should therefore be resisted in British English.

Nowadays, all major UK dictionary houses show **ize** and its derivatives as the preferred form. This is not to say that **ise** is incorrect, as it certainly is not; many newspapers still prefer this form. You will have noticed that this book follows the style of the dictionary house rather than the newspaper, and uses **ize** rather than **ise**.

When writing, it is important to be consistent with your choice, whether you opt for **ize** or **ise**. Pick one style and then stick to it. For example:

agonize or *agonise*
realization or *realisation*
organizer or *organiser*

Exceptions: there are a number of words that are always spelt with ise. These are:

advertise	**chastise**
advise	**circumcise**
apprise	**comprise**

compromise	franchise
demise	improvise
despise	incise
devise	premise
disenfranchise	prise (force open)
disfranchise	revise
disguise	supervise
enfranchise	surmise
excise	surprise
exercise	televise

There are also certain words that are always spelt with **ize**. These are:

capsize
prize (consider to be valuable)

Given that the words that must always end with **ise** outnumber those that must always end with **ize** by 13 to 1, it is easier to use the **ise** spelling as you will only have two exceptions to worry about.

Exercise

Some words must *always* be spelt with **ize** and some must *always* be spelt with **ise**. Which of the following are correct and which are incorrect?

1 Who ever thought it would be interesting to **televise** parliament?
2 We need to **devize** a new sales strategy.
3 She asked me to **supervise** her students while she was on holiday.
4 America and China both need to **compromise** if there is to be an agreement on climate change.
5 I ended up trying to **prize** the drawer open with a kitchen knife.
6 He plans to **disguise** himself and sneak into his ex-girlfriend's wedding.
7 In the new year I intend to **exercize** three times a week.
8 Do you think it would be expensive to **advertise** on the radio?
9 The idea is to turn up at his office and **surprise** him.
10 I **prize** my independence too much to get married and settle down.

10-question diagnostic test

1 *What do you add to a noun that ends with* **x** *to make it plural?*
2 *What are the possible plural endings for nouns that end with* **eau**?
3 *Can you think of four common nouns ending with* **o** *that add* **es** *to make their plurals?*
4 *Which letter do you add after* **c** *before adding an ending like* **er** *or* **y**?
5 *When an* **antenna** *is on an insect, what is its plural?*
6 *If a Scot calls one Englishman a* **Sassenach**, *what does he call two of them?*
7 *Which of these does not double its final consonant before adding* **ing**: **mop, develop, eavesdrop**?
8 *What is the past tense of the verb* **mislay**?
9 *What is the sound that* **ie** *and* **ei** *have to make for the rule about 'i before* **e** *except after* **c**' *to work?*
10 *Which of these words should never be spelt with* **ize**: **memorise, compartmentalise, despise**?

10 THINGS TO REMEMBER

1 *Most nouns take* **s** *or* **es** *when they become plural.*

2 *You add* **er** *to an adjective to make the comparative form.*

3 *You add* **est** *to an adjective to make the superlative form.*

4 *You add* **s** *or* **es** *to make the third person singular present tense of a verb.*

5 *You add* **ing** *to make the present participle of a verb.*

6 *You add* **d** *or* **ed** *to make the past tense of a verb.*

7 *Some words double their final consonant before adding an ending.*

8 *Sometimes* **y** *changes to* **i** *before adding an ending.*

9 *It is '***i** *before* **e** *except after* **c***'.*

10 *The ending* **ize** *is not just for Americans.*

5

Full stops and capital letters and apostrophes and hyphens and accents – oh my

In this chapter you will learn:
- *how to use full stops and capital letters correctly*
- *about the correct use of the apostrophe for possession and missing letters*
- *about the correct use of hyphens for split words and joined words*
- *how to use accents*
- *about the conventions for writing numbers.*

If you panic at the thought of punctuation, don't worry. This chapter isn't about commas and semicolons and colons. It's about the punctuation marks that relate to spelling – when to use them and when not.

Full stops and capitals and the rest may seem a bit, well, trivial. You might wonder why it matters if a word has a capital letter or a hyphen. The answer to that is that it matters because these punctuation marks contribute to the overall impression that people get from your writing. As I mentioned back in Chapter 1, it's important to spell words correctly because to do otherwise is to risk leading people to think that you are lazy, careless and not very smart. Correct punctuation is another aspect of correct spelling and the good news is that it's not hard to get it right.

Full stops

The full stop (.), also known as a *stop* or, in American English, a *period*, is used mainly to mark the end of a sentence, for example:

I am going to New York for Christmas.

In the past, full stops were used within abbreviations and acronyms, for example:

Mrs.	*U.S.A.*	*km.*
Dr.	*U.N.I.C.E.F.*	*etc.*
R.A.F.	*A.D.*	*e.g.*

But this practice is dying out as most people prefer a less fussy, cleaner look, so these are now typically written as:

Mrs	*USA*	*km*
Dr	*UNICEF*	*etc*
RAF	*AD*	*eg*

Exception: The abbreviation **a.m.** (for *ante meridiem*) which means 'before noon' or 'in the morning' is usually written with two full stops in order to avoid confusion with **am**, the first person singular present tense of the verb 'be'. Correspondingly, **p.m.** (for *post meridiem*), which means 'after noon', is often written with the two full stops, although it can also be written without, as there is no word **pm** with which it can be confused.

Capital letters

Proper names should always start with a capital letter. Proper names are the names of people, places, organizations, companies, animals, particular products, religious festivals, and so on, for example:

David Rawlings	*Channel 4*
Queen Mary	*Lassie*
Antarctica	*Pegasus*
Jupiter	*Pot Noodle*
The Verdant Works	*Red Bull*
World Wildlife Fund	*Christmas*
Plain English Campaign	*Diwali*
Heinz	

Words that are derived from the names of people and places should also start with a capital letter, for example:

Shakespearean	*Irish*
Freudian	*Liverpudlian*
Marxism	*African*
Calvinist	*Polynesian*

The first word in a sentence should start with a capital letter, for example:

There was an explosion and then the kitchen lights went out.
Girls can join the Scouts but boys can't join the Guides.
Next year Easter will be in April.

In recent years a trend has developed for what could be described as Random Capitalization. This happens very often in official or semi-official documents such as correspondence from public bodies, for example councils, political parties, providers of utilities like electricity, gas, water and telephone – and even advertising leaflets that get pushed through your letterbox, inviting you to build a new conservatory or replace your windows. These letters and adverts are full of words with unnecessary initial capitals, for example:

Dear Resident

**Your Local Council has been working in Partnership
with leading Businesses to find new and exciting ways**

to improve your Community. After many months of
Consultation we are delighted to announce our new
Sponsorship Plan.

A copy of the Plan is available on our Website and we
will be holding a Public Meeting at the beginning of March,
to which all Residents are invited. Further details will be
announced in the local Press nearer the time.

D Wilson
Business Development Unit Manager
North Southwood Council

In this trend, nouns (like **Partnership** and **Businesses**) and noun
phrases (like **Local Council** and **Public Meeting**) are written with
initial capitals which are quite unnecessary. It is generally nouns that
are given the Random Capitalization treatment. It is to be assumed
that it is done in order to stress the importance of certain words in
the letter or article, but the effect is actually the reverse: too many
capitals make it hard to tell what is important in a piece of writing.

The letter above would be better as follows:

Dear Resident

Your local council has been working in partnership
with leading businesses to find new and exciting ways
to improve your community. After many months of
consultation we are delighted to announce our new
Sponsorship Plan.

A copy of the plan is available on our website and we
will be holding a public meeting at the beginning of
March, to which all residents are invited. Further details
will be announced in the local press nearer the time.

D Wilson
Business Development Unit Manager
North Southwood Council

In this version, apart from the first word in a sentence, initial capitals are limited to the following:

▶ **Dear** – *the opening 'Dear' in a letter should always start with a capital*
▶ **Resident** – *the letter is addressed to this person, and the addressee should be capitalized as it would be if it were an individual name, such as Mrs Anderson or Mr Thomas*
▶ **Sponsorship Plan** – *as an official document (and assuming this is its title) it is acceptable to capitalize these words, as you would with the title of any official report, for example* The Chilcot Inquiry *or* The World Health Report
▶ **March** – *months of the year and days of the week should always start with a capital letter*
▶ **D Wilson** – *this is the person signing the letter*
▶ **Business Development Unit Manager** – *this is a job title, so the individual words can be capitalized*
▶ **North Southwood Council** – *this is the name of the organization.*

When you are writing something and are tempted to use a capital, ask yourself the following questions:

▶ *Is this the proper or official name of a person, place or thing?*
▶ *Is this the beginning of a sentence?*
▶ *Is it the day of the week or the month of the year?*
▶ *Is it a word that describes a nationality or religion?*

If the answer to each of these is 'no', then think twice before putting that capital letter there.

Exercise

The following passage contains unnecessary capital letters, as well as small letters where there ought to be capitals. Can you spot the mistakes?

This christmas i am going to the Wedding of my friends Douglas and angela. It will be held in a Hotel in the South

Side of Glasgow, and I expect to see a lot of people I have not seen since Last Year. The whole wedding will be taking place in the Hotel, and the Minister is coming up from Ayrshire to perform the Ceremony. The weather forecast on the BBC last night said that there is a good chance there will be snow on Christmas day. That would be lovely for the photographs but i just hope that all the Guests will be able to get here. Will I have to wear my Wellies under my dress?

Apostrophes

The apostrophe has two main functions:

- ▶ *to indicate possession or ownership*
- ▶ *to show that at least one letter is missing.*

THE APOSTROPHE AND POSSESSION

The apostrophe is used after a noun to show that the following thing or things (or person or people) belong to the noun. The apostrophe is followed by an s, for example:

Eve's bedroom (= the bedroom of Eve)
George's basket (= the basket of George)
Anna's three brothers (= the three brothers of Anna)
my sister's husband (= the husband of my sister)
the postman's bag (= the bag of the postman)
your car's windscreen (= the windscreen of your car)

When the noun is plural and ends with s, you add the apostrophe after the final s, for example:

the teachers' Christmas party (= the Christmas party of the teachers)
your parents' friends (= the friends of your parents)
my horses' saddles (= the saddles of my horses)
the aeroplanes' wings (= the wings of the aeroplanes)

If the noun is a plural that does not end with s, you add the apostrophe and letter **s** at the end of the word, for example:

our children's future (= the future of our children)
men's fashion (= fashion for men)
the people's decision (= the decision of the people)

> ## Insight
> Remember to think before you write **it's** and **its**. **Its** is a possessive pronoun, used for things like 'the horse broke **its** leg' and 'the country has lost **its** way'. **It's** is short for 'it is' and 'it has', so is used in sentences like '**it's** been freezing cold for three weeks now' and '**it's** incredibly annoying when people put apostrophes where they shouldn't be'.

THE APOSTROPHE AND THE MISSING LETTER

An apostrophe in a word can also be a sign that at least one letter has been omitted, and that the word is two words joined together, for example:

I'm (= I am)
I've (= I have)
I'll (= I will or I shall)
he's (= he is or he has)
you'd (= you had or you would)
they're (= they are)
it's (= it is or it has)
can't (= cannot)
won't (= will not)
didn't (= did not)

APOSTROPHES AND PLURALS

Do you use an apostrophe to make a plural? The answer is **NO!**

The famous (or infamous) greengrocer's apostrophe refers to the way that some plurals of fruit and vegetables are written on signs outside these shops, for example:

Fresh apple's, orange's and pear's!
Cauliflower's and cabbage's just in!
Raspberry's and strawberry's on special offer!

This is wrong. You do *not* make a plural form of a noun by adding an apostrophe and an s. These announcements should be written as:

Fresh apples, oranges and pears!
Cauliflowers and cabbages just in!
Raspberries and strawberries on special offer!

Even abbreviations do not have an apostrophe in the plural form, for example:

CD → CDs
DVD → DVDs
LP → LPs
ISP → ISPs
MP → MPs
ATM → ATMs
IOU → IOUs

Exception: There is only one exception to the rule about apostrophes, and that is when you are writing the plural of an individual letter of the alphabet and only then when it is a small letter (as opposed to a capital letter), for example:

You will need to watch your p's *and q*'s *in this new job.*
They will expect you to dot all the i's *and cross all the t*'s.
Remember that 'accommodate' has two c's *and two m*'s.

Hyphens

A hyphen is a short line (-) that does two different things. It joins separate words together and it shows the place where a single word has been split. The verb **to hyphenate** means 'to insert or join with a hyphen'.

SPLIT WORDS

When you are typing a document and there are too many letters to fit into the line, the words run on to the next line. If you have fixed the width of the document so that all the lines are the same length (this is called *justified* text), sometimes a word will have to be split into order to avoid an awkward-looking gap in a line. Your word-processing package will do this for you. It will split a word at an appropriate point and insert a hyphen at the end of the first part of the word, in order to show that the group of letters at the start of the following line are actually the end of the previous word.

Different word-processing and typesetting packages have their own rules about where it is correct (and incorrect) to hyphenate a word. These rules are either based on the etymology (that is, the origin) of the word, in which case a Latin or Greek root in a word would never be split in two: for example, the word **terracotta** could not be split between the two **r**'s, because *terra* is a Latin root word meaning 'earth'. By this rule, the only acceptable place to split **terracotta** is between the **a** and the **c**: terra- and **cotta**.

Other packages will split words according to the syllables, in which case **terracotta** can be split in three places: between **ter-** and **ra-**, between **ra-** and **cot-** and between and **cot-** and **ta**.

In most cases, you, as the writer, will not have to make any decisions about where or not to split a word, as it is decided for you by your word processor.

However, if for some reason you do have to make a decision about where to split a word that is to be broken over two lines, here are a few simple rules to help you:

- ▶ *Don't split a word after the first letter (*a-griculture*)*
- ▶ *Don't split a word before the final letter (***agricultur-e***)*
- ▶ *Don't split a person's name (***Dav-id Beck-ham***)*
- ▶ *Don't split a word that is already hyphenated (***left-hand-ed***)*
- ▶ *Don't split a word in a place that makes another word (***mate-rial***)*

JOINED WORDS

You are much more likely to be using a hyphen to join two words to make a new word than you are to be using it to split an existing word. Words in English can be in three states:

1 *separate words* (**red eye** = *the effect in a photograph when the flash makes the eyes appear red*)
2 *hyphenated word* (**red-eye** = *an aeroplane flight that leaves late at night and arrives early the next morning*)
3 *solid word* (**redeye** = *a slang word in American English for cheap whisky*).

It is pretty unusual for there to be three words like this: one separate, one hyphenated and one solid, all from the same two words, and all with different meanings. But it is very common for there to be pairs of words like this, with each one of the pair having a different part of speech, for example:

line up (verb) and *line-up (noun)*
break down (verb) and *breakdown (noun)*
run in (verb) and *run-in (noun)*
broad spectrum (noun) and *broad-spectrum (adjective)*

There are simple rules that help you know when a word should be hyphenated or not.

Verbs
Some verbs are always used with a preposition or adverb, for example:

break away
look in
pick up
turn over

When you write a verb like this, you do not put a hyphen between the verb and its preposition or adverb.

Nouns and adjectives from verbs

Many of these verbs have nouns and adjectives that are made from them, so from the above examples we have:

breakaway (noun and adjective)
look-in (noun)
pick-up (noun and adjective)
turnover (noun and adjective)

These are either formed by hyphenating the two words, or by combining them into one solid word. There is no rule about which verbs follow which style in this and, in fact, different dictionaries will even show you different styles. The truth is that this area of language is very fluid and changeable. However, the trend in language is always away from separate words, towards a hyphenated form, and then, finally, to a solid word. A good example of this trend (although not one from a verb) is the word **airmail**. Originally written as two words (**air mail**) it gradually became more common to write the hyphenated form **air-mail**. And nowadays it is almost universally written as one solid word: **airmail**.

The good thing is that there is no 'wrong' way to write an adjective or noun from one of these verbs, as long as you make it either hyphenated or solid. Check your dictionary and be sure to keep it consistent within your writing.

Making adjectives

If you have an adjective (like **first**) that is referring to a noun (like **night**), together these make a noun phrase (**first night**). To make an adjective from one of these noun phrases, you join the words with a hyphen (**first-night**):

Noun	Adjective	Example
common law	common-law	common-law wife
broad spectrum	broad-spectrum	broad-spectrum antibiotic
open door	open-door	open-door policy
heavy metal	heavy-metal	heavy-metal music
multiple choice	multiple-choice	multiple-choice questions

Noun	Adjective	Example
blue rinse	blue-rinse	blue-rinse brigade
front page	front-page	front-page news

The same rule applies when you combine a noun or adverb with a present participle or a past participle, for example:

Noun/Adverb	Present/Past Participle	Adjective
gin	swilling	gin-swilling
cheese	eating	cheese-eating
long	suffering	long-suffering
tough	talking	tough-talking
rain	sodden	rain-sodden
hate	filled	hate-filled
never	forgotten	never-forgotten
often	married	often-married

There are a number of adjectives consisting of two or more words that are sometimes hyphenated and sometimes not. The use of the hyphen depends on where the adjective comes in relation to the person or thing it is describing. Take, for example, the adjective **up to the minute**. If the adjective comes after its subject (the thing it describes), there is no need to put hyphens between the words, as in:

This news report is **up to the minute**.

But if you put the adjective in front of the subject, you put hyphens between the words, as in:

Now let's have an **up-to-the-minute** *report from our foreign correspondent.*

This rule applies to the many adjectives formed with the adverb **well**, for example:

After its subject	Before its subject
well adjusted	well-adjusted
well behaved	well-behaved

(Contd)

After its subject	Before its subject
well deserved	well-deserved
well fed	well-fed
well heeled	well-heeled
well kept	well-kept
well liked	well-liked
well off	well-off
well prepared	well-prepared
well read	well-read
well spoken	well-spoken
well thought of	well-thought-of

Insight

Some writers take the hyphenated-adjective convention to extremes in order to create a comic effect, for example:

sandal-wearing-brown-rice-eating-long-haired-peace-loving-anti-nuclear-Guardian-reading liberals.

Exercise

In the following passage some words ought to be hyphenated, some ought to be separate and some ought to be solid. Do you know which is which?

The start of a new year is traditionally the time to turnover a new leaf and make resolutions about the things you will do better or give-up. These often relate to health-issues like smoking, diet and exercise. I plan to take-up running again with the aim of competing in a ten kilometre race next May. It is for women only. Last year almost 15,000 people took-part. I some times find it hard to make myself go out on a cold winter's night, but I know I'll feel more up-for-it when the days get longer in the run up to the race. A few of my well off friends are members of the posh gym near here but I have never enjoyed exercising in-doors.

Accented letters

An accent is a mark over a letter that shows that it is to be pronounced in a particular way. Most English words that have accents have come from other languages, especially French, Spanish and German.

ACUTE ACCENT

The acute or acute accent is a short straight line that rises from left to right (´). Its use in English shows that a word is of French origin, and it appears over the letter e, for example:

attaché	divorcé and divorcée	risqué
		rosé
blasé	éclair	
		sauté
café	fiancé and fiancée	séance
cliché		Sémillon
coupé	née	soufflé
décor	protégé	touché

Insight

If you can't remember which accent is the acute and which is the grave, here is a mnemonic I was taught at school:

One rainy day a man was walking past Glasgow Academy and his umbrella blew inside out.

Now imagine the inverted V shape of an inside-out umbrella between the letters G and A (G V A). The half of the V shape nearest the G is a grave (the line falling from left to right) and the half nearest the A is the acute (the line rising from left to right). Feel free to change Glasgow Academy to any other institution with the initials GA.

GRAVE ACCENT

The grave or grave accent is a short straight line that falls from left to right (`). Its use in English shows that a word is of French origin, and it appears over the letters **a** and **e**, for example:

à la carte   *cortège*
à la mode   *crèche*
après-ski   *première*
brassière   *son et lumière*
cafetière   *vis-à-vis*

CIRCUMFLEX

The circumflex is an accent that looks like a flattened, upside-down **v** (^). Its use in English shows that a word is of French origin, and it appears over the letters **a**, **e** and **o**, for example:

arête   *pâtisserie*
fête   *table d'hôte*
papier-mâché   *tête-à-tête*
pâté

Insight
The circumflex in French words often shows where there was originally a letter **s** that became silent. Take **hotel** and **hostel** as examples. **Hostel** is an Old French word that came into English in the thirteenth century. **Hotel** came into English in the seventeenth century from the French word *hôtel*, which is the original Old French word *hostel* without its **s**, with the loss indicated by a circumflex.

TILDE

The tilde is an accent that looks like a squiggly line (˜). Its use in English shows that a word is of Spanish origin, and it appears over the letter **n**, for example:

El Niño
jalapeño
mañana
piña colada

piñata
Señor and *Señora* and *Señorita*
vicuña

UMLAUT

The umlaut is an accent that looks like two dots (¨). Its use in English shows that a word is of German origin, and it appears over the letters **a, o** and **u,** for example:

Fräulein
Führer
jäger
ländler
röntgen

This mark is also called a diaeresis or dieresis. It is called this when it is placed over the second of two vowels in a row, and it shows that the second vowel is to be pronounced separately from the first vowel, for example:

Noël
naïve
Chloë
Zoë

Confusingly, the same mark is used for an umlaut and a diaeresis. However, apart from these few words, the diaeresis is extremely rare in modern English.

CEDILLA

The cedilla is a small hook (¸) that appears under the letter **c** in words of French origin. The cedilla indicates that the **c** is pronounced like **s** rather than **k,** in such words as:

aperçu
façade

garçon
soupçon

Of the four, **façade** is by far the commonest in English and has become so well established that the Anglicized spelling **facade**, without the cedilla, is also considered to be correct.

The cedilla is also used in Catalan and its use may be familiar to you through the word **Barça**, a diminutive name for Barcelona FC.

Numbers

The writing of numbers often causes problems. Should you write them in words or figures? Should they have commas or hyphens or spaces or nothing at all? Below is a simple explanation of the conventions that apply to the writing of numbers.

ONE TO TWELVE

The convention is to write the numbers from one to twelve in words, not figures:

one	*seven*
two	*eight*
three	*nine*
four	*ten*
five	*eleven*
six	*twelve*

13 TO INFINITY

From 13 onwards you use figures, not words:

13
14
15
100

1000
1,000,000

When you are writing a number that is greater than 9999 – for example, 10,000 and upwards – you should use commas to make the number easier to read. The comma is used to mark off every group of three figures from the right of the number, so:

10,000
1,000,000
1,000,000,000

Insight

You do not need to use a comma for the numbers between 1000 and 9999 inclusive. So you should not write 1,000 or 5,690. These numbers should be written 1000 and 5690.

You do not use a comma after a decimal point:

1,000,000.0000001

But if a number comes at the beginning of a sentence you should write it in words rather than figures, for example:

One million people are currently living in poverty in our inner cities.

10-question diagnostic text

1 *Can you name one abbreviation that still has full stops?*
2 *What are the two functions of the apostrophe?*
3 *When is the only time you can use an apostrophe to make a plural of a noun?*
4 *Which letters can have a grave accent?*
5 *Which letters can have a circumflex?*
6 *Which letter can have a tilde?*
7 *Which letter can have a cedilla?*
8 *Which letter can have an acute accent?*
9 *Which letters can have an umlaut?*
10 *Which letters can have a diaeresis?*

10 THINGS TO REMEMBER

1 Correct punctuation is an important part of good spelling.

2 Restrict your use of initial capital letters to proper names and the first word in a sentence.

3 Most abbreviations and acronyms are written without full stops.

4 You do not use apostrophes to make plural nouns.

5 You do not put a hyphen between a verb and the adverb or preposition that goes with it.

6 You put a hyphen between two words to make them into an adjective.

7 If the adjective comes after the things it describes, it does not need to have a hyphen.

8 The commonest accents are the acute, grave, tilde, circumflex, cedilla and umlaut.

9 You should write the numbers one to twelve in words.

10 You should write the numbers 13 and over in figures.

6

Problem words

In this chapter you will learn:
- *the most commonly misspelt words in English*
- *possible reasons why they are problematic*
- *some techniques for practising these tricky words.*

Below you will find a list of 900 of the most commonly misspelt words in English.

It is highly unlikely that you will have problems remembering the correct spelling of all of them. You may look at many of them and wonder how anyone could find them difficult to spell. But everyone has their blind spots. (And I mean everyone: mine are **privilege** and **sacrilege**. I had to check them again just there). But the following list includes most of the words that are, for one reason or another, often spelt incorrectly. The reason could be a double letter (as in **accelerate**); a single letter where you might expect a double letter (as in **aficionado**); a silent letter (as in **abscess**); or a misleading similarity to another word (as with **religious** and **sacrilegious**). Have a good look at this list. Identifying the words that you find tricky is an essential step on the road to better spelling.

Most commonly misspelt words in English

abscess
absence
abundance
accelerate
acceptable
accessible
accessory
accidentally
acclaim
accommodate
accommodation
accomplish
accordion
accumulate
achieve
achievement
acknowledge
acknowledgement
acquaintance
acquire
acquit
across
address
adieu
adjacent
adultery
advertise
advertisement
advisable
aerosol
aesthetic
aficionado
aggravate
aggression
aggressive
alcohol

allege
allegiance
alphabet
amateur
ameliorate
among
anaesthesia
anaesthetic
analyse
analysis
anemone
anoint
annually
Antarctic
antonym
apartheid
apartment
apparatus
apparent
appearance
apropos
aqueduct
arbitrary
Arctic
argument
artefact
ascend
atheist
athlete
athletic
attendance
auspicious
autumn
average
awful

bachelor
bait
balance
balloon
barbecue
bargain
baroque
basically
beautiful
because
becoming
before
beggar
beginning
beguile
beige
belief
believe
bellwether
beneficial
benefit
besiege
bias
biscuit
bivouac
boudoir
boundary
boycott
brief
brilliant
broccoli
Buddhist
budget
buoy
buoyant
bureaucracy

burglar
business

calendar
camouflage
candidate
cappuccino
careful
Caribbean
cartridge
catalogue
category
caught
ceiling
cemetery
ceremony
certain
challenge
changeable
character
characteristic
chauffeur
chief
chocolate
choir
chord
chorus
cigarette

cinnamon
cipher
citizen
cognac
cognoscenti
coiffure
colleague
collectible
colonel
colony
colour
column
comfortable
commandment
commemorate
commiserate
commission
commit
commitment
committed
committee
comparative
competent
competition
completely
concede
conceive
condemn

condescend
congratulate
connoisseur
conscience
conscientious
conscious
consensus
consistent
contemporary
continuous
contour
controversy
convenient
coolly
correlate
correspond
correspondence
courteous
courtesy
criticism
criticize
crotchet
current
curriculum
cursor
cycle

Insight

The **dahlia** is named after the Swedish botanist Anders Dahl who first discovered it in Mexico in the late eighteenth century. The expression **blue dahlia** refers to something rare or nonexistent, because dahlias are never blue.

dahlia
daiquiri
deceive
decide

decipher
defendant
definite
definitely

depend
dependent
deposit
descend

describe
description
desiccate
desirable
despair
desperate
develop
dialysis
diamond
diarrhoea
diary
dictionary
difference
digit
dilemma
director
disappear
disappearance
disappoint
disaster

disastrous
disciple
discipline
dissatisfied
dominant
drunkenness
dumbbell
during
dynasty

easel
easily
ecclesiastical
economic
ecstasy
effervescent
effete
efficiency
efficient
eighth

either
element
eligible
eliminate
emaciate
embarrass
emigrant
emperor
encouragement
encyclopedia
enemy
entente
enthral
entrepreneur
environment
epistle
equipment
espionage
espresso

Insight

Espresso is strong coffee made by forcing boiling water or steam through ground beans. It comes from *caffè espresso* which is literally the Italian for 'pressed coffee'.

eulogy
euphemism
euphoria
euthanasia
eviscerate
exacerbate
exaggerate
exceed
excerpt
exercise
exhilarate
existence
expect

expense
experience
experiment
explanation
extraneous
extraordinary
extraterrestrial
extravagant
extreme
extrovert
exuberance

facade
facetious
facsimile
fallacious
falsetto
familiar
fantasy
fascinate
feasible
February
fetus
fictitious
field

fierce
fiery
finally
financially
flour
fluorescent
foreign
foresee
forfeit
forty

forward
four
fourth
freeze
friend
frieze
fulfil
fundamental
funeral
furore

garrotte
gateau
gauge
generally
generosity
generous
genius
genre
glamorous
glamour

Insight

Glamour is a Scots variant of **grammar** that was popularized by Sir Walter Scott. Its original meaning was 'a magic spell' because magic and the occult were traditionally associated with education and learning, and therefore with grammar.

glossary
gorgeous
gourmet
government
graffiti
grammar
grateful
grievous
guarantee
guard
guardian
guerrilla
guess
guidance
guile

haemorrhage
haemorrhoids
halcyon
hallelujah
hamster
handkerchief

harass
hazard
height
heinous
hesitant
hierarchy
hindrance
Hindu
honorary
honour
humorous
humour
hygiene
hymn
hypnotic
hypocrisy

ideally
identity
idiosyncrasy
ignorance
illegible

imaginary
imitate
imitation
immediate
immediately
immigrant
implement
impresario
inadvertent
incidentally
independence
independent
indict
indispensable
inevitable
innocuous
inoculate
inseparable
instalment
integrate
intelligence
interesting

interfere
internet
interpretation
interrupt
interruption

invitation
introvert
involve
irregular
irrelevant

irresistible
irritable
island

Insight

The word **island** comes from the Old English *īgland*. It later became *īland*. The **s** was inserted in the sixteenth century through association with the word **isle**, an Old French word, which had been in English since the thirteenth century.

isosceles
itinerary

jaundice
jealous
jeopardy
jewellery
judgement
judicial
jugular
jurisdiction
juvenile

kaleidoscope
karaoke
kernel
kerosene
kilogram
knowledge
knowledgeable

label
laboratory
lackadaisical
languor
latitude
league

legitimate
leisure
length
liaise
liaison
librarian
library
lieutenant
lightning
likelihood
liquefy
liquid
litre
loneliness
longitude
lugubrious
luminescent
lyric

macabre
machine
maelstrom
magazine
maintain
maintenance
maisonette
malign

malleable
manageable
manoeuvre
manufacture
margarine
marriage
masquerade
massacre
mathematics
mayonnaise
medicine
medieval
Mediterranean
melody
memento
memory
menstruate
meretricious
metamorphosis
metaphor
metre
millennium
millionaire
miniature
minus
minuscule
miracle

miscellaneous
mischief
mischievous
misdemeanour
misogynist
missile
misspell
moccasin
modem
monitor
moreover
mortgage
mosquito
movement
murmur

muscle
mysterious
myth

naive
narrative
narrator
naturally
nauseate
nauseous
necessary
necessity
negligible
neighbour
nervous

neurosis
niece
ninety
ninth
noticeable
novel
nuisance
numerator

obedience
obsequious
obscene
obsess
obstacle
obstreperous

Insight

The adjective **obstreperous**, which means 'rough or noisy, or resisting control', came into English in the sixteenth century from the Latin *obstrepere*, which itself comes from *ob* meaning 'against' and *strepere* meaning 'to roar'. So it literally means 'roaring against'.

occasion
occasionally
occur
occurred
occurrence
ochre
official
often
omelette
omission
onomatopoeia
opaque
operate
ophthalmic
opinion
opponent

opportunity
oppression
optimism
optimistic
orchestra
ordinarily
ordinary
origin
original
ought
outrageous
overrun
oxygen

pamphlet
parable

paradigm
paraffin
paragraph
parallel
parallelogram
paralysis
paraphernalia
paraplegia
parliament
particular
particularly
pastel
pastime
pattern
pavilion
peccadillo

peculiar
pedagogue
penchant
people
penetrate
perceive
perform
performance
perimeter
permanent
permissible

pernicious
perpendicular
persevere
perseverance
persistence
persistent
perspective
perspicacious
perspiration
persuade
pharaoh

pharmaceutical
philanthropy
phlegm
phraseology
physical
physician
picaresque
picture
picturesque

Insight

The word **picaresque** is sometimes confused with **picturesque** although there is no connection between them. **Picaresque** describes a type of writing in which a roguish hero has a series of adventures. It comes from the Spanish *pícaro* which means 'a rogue'.

piece
pigeon
pilgrimage
piquant
pitiful
plagiarize
playwright
pleasant
poignant
political
pollution
polyester
portfolio
portrait
portray
possession
possibility
possible
practical
practically

prairie
precede
precedence
predator
prefer
preferable
preference
prejudice
premises
preparation
prerogative
prescription
presence
prevalent
priest
primitive
privilege
probably
process
profession

professional
professor
proletariat
prominent
promise
pronounce
pronunciation
proof
propaganda
protein
Protestant
provincial
psychedelic
psychiatry
psychology
pubescent
publicly
pursue

quantity
quarantine
quarter
questionnaire
queue
quintessential

racism
raconteur
rapport
rapprochement
raspberry
ratatouille
readable
realistically
reality
realize
really
recede
receipt
receive
recipe

recognize
recommend
reconnaissance
recoup
recur
refer
reference
referred
refrigerator
reign
relevance
relevant
relief
relieve
religion
religious
remember
remembrance
reminiscent
rendezvous
repetition
research

resemblance
reservoir
resistance
restaurant
restaurateur
resuscitate
rhetoric
rheumatism
rhinoceros
rhombus
rhyme
rhythm
rhythmic
ricochet
ridiculous
risotto
rural

sabotage
saboteur
sacrifice
sacrilege

Insight

Sacrilege is the act of misusing something sacred. It came into English from the Old French word *sacrilège*, which is derived from the Latin *sacra* meaning 'sacred things' and *legere* meaning 'to take'. A *sacrilegus* was a temple-robber: that is a person who took sacred things.

sacrilegious
safety
salary
sandal
sanctimonious
satellite
Saturday
sausage

scenario
scene
scenery
schedule
schizophrenic
scissors
secondary
secretary

seismic
seize
sensible
sentence
separate
sepulchre
sergeant
series

several
shepherd
shoulder
siege
sieve
sign
Sikh
silhouette
similar
simile
simultaneous
sincere
sixth
skiing
skilful
soldier
soliloquy
sorbet
source
souvenir
sovereign
special
specifically
specimen
spectrum
speech
sponsor
spontaneous
stereotype
stomach
straight
strategy
strength
strenuous
subtle
succeed
success
sufficient

sulphur
supercilious
supersede
suppress
surprise
surreptitious
surround
susceptible
suspicious
sycophant
syllable
symbol
symmetrical
symmetry
synagogue
synchronize
syncopation
synonym
synthesize
system

tactic
tangible
technical
technique
technology
temperamental
temperature
temporary
tendency
tertiary
textile
theatre
thermometer
thesaurus
threshold
through
tomorrow

tongue
tourist
tournament
towards
traitor
triangle
triangular
tragedy
truly
twelfth
tyranny
tyrant

ubiquitous
ukulele
ululate
umbilical
unanimous
unconscious
unctuous
underrate
undoubtedly
undulate
unforgettable
unfortunately
unguent
unique
unnecessary
until
upholstery
usable
usual
uxorious

vaccinate
vacillate
vacuum
vague

variegated	veterinary	vocabulary
vegetable	vicious	volume
vegetarian	vigilant	
vehement	village	waive
vehicle	villain	warrant
vengeance	virtue	weather
vertebrate	virus	Wednesday
vertical	viscous	weight
vestige	vitamin	weird

Insight

Although **weird** now has the meaning of 'eerie' or 'bizarre', its original meaning was 'relating to fate'. It comes from the Anglo-Saxon word *wyrd*, which means 'destiny'. That is why Macbeth's three witches are also known as 'the weird sisters': they know what Macbeth's destiny is. They are quite strange too.

welcome	xenophobia	zealous
welfare	xylophone	zephyr
wholly		zeppelin
wilful	yacht	zucchini
withhold	yeoman	
worthwhile	yield	
writing	yoghurt	

Exercise

It's a good idea to practise these tricky words. Break the list down into manageable chunks, either by letter or something smaller like groups of thirty. If you have an obliging friend or child, get them to read the words out to you and see if you can spell them. If you can't find anyone willing to help, you could record them into a Dictaphone or a mobile phone and play them back when you have some spare time. If your particular problem word isn't mentioned above, add it to the list.

(Contd)

Look closely at the words. Can you work out why each of them could cause problems? Think about the reasons given at the start of the chapter, for example double letters, single letters, silent letters, odd letter combinations, and similarities to but differences from other words.

10-question diagnostic test

1 *Why do you think people often spell 'graffiti' incorrectly?*
2 *Why do you think people often spell 'bivouac' incorrectly?*
3 *Why do you think people often spell 'vacuum' incorrectly?*
4 *Why do you think people often spell 'aficionado' incorrectly?*
5 *Why do you think people often spell 'subtle' incorrectly?*
6 *Why do you think people often spell 'refrigerator' incorrectly?*
7 *Why do you think people often spell 'welfare' incorrectly?*
8 *Why do you think people often spell 'desiccate' incorrectly?*
9 *Why do you think people often spell 'restaurateur' incorrectly?*
10 *Why do you think people often spell 'impresario' incorrectly?*

10 THINGS TO REMEMBER

1 *Look out for single letters where you might expect double letters.*

2 *Look out for double letters where you might expect single letters.*

3 *Look out for silent letters.*

4 *Look out for odd combinations of letters.*

5 *Do not let the spelling of one word influence how you think another is spelt.*

6 *Check the list to identify the words you know you have problems spelling.*

7 *Practise your problem words regularly.*

8 *Ask a friend to quiz you on them or record them into your mobile phone or into a Dictaphone.*

9 *Get into the habit of checking your problem words when you write them.*

10 *Add any other words that you struggle with to this list.*

7

English in pieces

In this chapter you will learn:
- *about the building blocks of English words: prefixes, suffixes and roots*
- *how becoming familiar with these building blocks will help with your spelling*
- *how becoming familiar with these will also help your understanding of written English.*

You should find that it helps your spelling to know some of the building blocks that are used to create English words. These building blocks are prefixes, suffixes and roots.

▶ A **prefix** *is a letter or group of letters added to the beginning of a word to add to or change its meaning.*
▶ A **suffix** *is a letter or group of letters added to the end of a word to add to or change its meaning.*
▶ A **root** *is a word from another language, often Latin or Greek, which can be used to create many different words.*

Insight
The word **suffix** comes from the Latin *suffixus* which means 'fastened below', from *sub* meaning 'beneath' and *figere* meaning 'to fasten'. *Prae* is Latin for 'before' so **prefix** means 'fastened before'.

The rules of English spelling in Chapter 4 of this book explain how adding suffixes affects the spelling of a word. This chapter explains what these affixes and roots mean, and give examples of each (an **affix** is a word that means a prefix or a suffix). If you become familiar with these words, it will help you with your spelling and it will also enhance your understanding (and hopefully enjoyment) of a wide range of styles of written English.

Prefixes

Word	Meaning	Examples
ab-	away, from	abnormal, absolve
ad-	to, towards	adjust, adverb
agri-, agro-	farming, fields	agriculture, agronomy
amphi-	both	amphibian
amphi-	around	amphitheatre
an-, a-	without, not	anaemia, asexual
andro-	male	androgynous, android
ante-	before	antenatal, anteroom
anti-	against	antifreeze, antisocial
arch-	chief	archbishop, archenemy
astro-	star	astronomy, astronaut
be-	thoroughly	besiege, bespatter
bi-	two, twice	bicycle, bilingual
cent-	hundred, hundredth	centenary, centimetre
chron-	time	chronometer, chronology
circ-	round	circumference, circuit
co-	with	cohabit, co-operate
contra-	against	contradict, contraception
cyber-	computer	cyberspace, cybercafé
de-	removal, reversal	delouse, defrost
deca-	ten	decade, decagon
deci-	tenth	decimal, decimate
di-	two, twice	diarchy, dicephalous

(Contd)

Word	Meaning	Examples
dis-	removal, reversal	disband, disempower
dys-	abnormal, faulty	dysfunctional, dyslexia
e-	of the internet	e-commerce, email
eco-	environment	ecology, ecosystem
electro-	electricity	electronic, electroplate
epi-, ep-	upon, over	epidermis, epidural
equ-	horse	equine, equestrian
equi-	equal	equinox, equidistant
ex-	out, outside, from	expel, extend
ex-	former	ex-wife, ex-serviceman
extra-	beyond	extraordinary, extramarital
for-	rejection	forbid, forswear
fore-	before, forward	foresee, forearm
frater-, fratri-	brother	fraternal, fratricide
geo-	earth	geography, geometry
haemo-	blood	haemorrhage, haemoglobin
hemi-	half	hemisphere, hemitrope
hepta-	seven	heptagon, heptathlon
hexa-	six	hexagon, hexameter
homeo-	like, similar	homeopathy, homeostasis
hyper-	above, excessive	hypercritical, hypersensitive
hypo-	under, deficient	hypodermic, hypoglycaemic
in-	not	inappropriate, incoherent
in-	in, into, towards	infiltrate, incarcerate
infra-	beneath	infrastructure, infrared
inter-	between, together	interface, intermarry
iso-	equal, identical	isobar, isosceles
kilo-	thousand	kilogram, kilowatt
macro-	large	macroeconomics, macroclimate

Word	Meaning	Examples
mater-, matri-	mother	maternal, matricide
mega-	large	megalith, megaphone
micro-	small	microphone, microorganism
mid-	middle	midland, midsummer
mini-	small, short	minicomputer, miniskirt
mis-	wrong, wrongly	misinform, misread
mono-, mon-	one	monolingual, monocle
multi-	many, much	multicoloured, multimedia
neo-	new	Neolithic, neonatal
neur-, neuro-	nerve, nervous system	neurosurgery, neural
non-	not	nonpayment, nonexistent
oct-	eight	octopus, octave
omni-	all	omnipotent, omniscient
ortho-, orth-	straight, correct	orthodox, orthodontist
over-	excessive, superior	overcharge, overlord
paedo-, paed-	child, children	paediatrics, paedophile
pan-	every	pantheism, pan-African
para-	near, resembling	parameter, paralegal
patho-	disease	pathology, pathogen
pater-, patri-	father	paternity, patriarch
penta-	five	pentagon, pentangle
per-	through	permit, permanent
peri-	around	perimeter, periphery
perma-	permanent	permafrost, perma-tan
poly-	many	polygamy, Polynesia
post-	after, behind	postgraduate, posterior
pre-	before	prejudge, prenuptial
pro-	favouring	pro-choice, pro-life
pyro-	fire	pyrotechnics, pyromania
quadr-	four	quadrilateral, quadruplet
quint-	five	quintet, quintuplet
re-	again	reapply, recollect
rhino-	nose	rhinoceros, rhinoplasty
self-	of oneself	self-employed, self-styled
semi-	half	semidetached, semicircle

(Contd)

Word	Meaning	Examples
sept-	seven	septet, septuplet
sex-	six	sextet, sextuplet
sub-	under	submarine, subheading
super-	above, very, large	supercilious, supercharge
syn-	together	synthesize, synchronize
techno-	technology	technocrat, technophobe
tele-	distant	television, telephone
theo-	God, gods	theology, theocentric
trans-	across, beyond	transform, transmit
tri-	three	triangle, triathlon
ultra-	beyond, extremely	ultrasonic, ultraviolet
un-	not, opposite	unmarried, untie
under-	beneath, less	underwear, underpaid
uni-	only one	unicycle, unilateral
vice-	deputy	vice-chairman, viceroy
web-	World Wide Web	webcam, webpage
zoo-	animal	zoology, zooplankton

Suffixes

Word	Meaning	Examples
-able	capable of	avoidable, enjoyable
-aholic, -oholic	addicted to	workaholic, chocoholic
-al	related to	musical, governmental
-ance	quality of, act of	abundance, compliance
-arch	ruler	matriarch, oligarch
-archy	government	anarchy, monarchy
-ary	related to	budgetary, complimentary
-ate	having, resembling	fortunate, lineate
-ate	become, take	validate, hyphenate
-ation	state of, action of	admiration, defamation
-athon, -thon	charity event	swimathon, telethon

Word	Meaning	Examples
-cian	profession of	politician, technician
-cide	murder of	suicide, matricide
-dom	state of, condition of	boredom, freedom
-dox	opinion, belief	orthodox, paradox
-en	become	weaken, toughen
-ence	state of, action of	occurrence, preference
-ent	causing	abhorrent, absorbent
-er	person that does	painter, builder
-er	tool that does	sharpener, dehumidifier
-er	person from	Icelander, northerner
-er	more	happier, quieter
-est	most	happiest, quietest
-ette	small	novelette, kitchenette
-ette	imitation	satinette, leatherette
-ferous	containing, bearing	oniferous, carboniferous
-fest	festival	songfest, gabfest

Insight

The suffix **-fest** is from German and it literally means 'festival'. It is quite often used in a jokey way, for example a *pizzafest*, a *crispfest* or a *boozefest*. Like the German Oktoberfest, these fests tend to suggest an element of overindulgence.

-free	without	carefree, fat-free
-ful	full of	spiteful, eventful
-fy	make, become	intensify, prettify
-gate	scandal	Watergate, boozegate

Insight

The original **-gate** was Watergate. This was the scandal that cost US president Richard Nixon his job, when it was discovered that he had been involved in an attempt to cover up a break-in at the Democratic headquarters in the Watergate Building in Washington. The -gate suffix continues to thrive.

Word	Meaning	Examples
-gon	mathematical figure	pentagon, polygon
-gram	written or drawn	cardiogram, anagram
-hedron	geometric solid	tetrahedron, octahedron
-hood	state of, condition of	widowhood, parenthood
-ible	able to	digestible, accessible
-ic	related to	acrobatic, demonic
-ication	state of, action of	mummification, justification
-ion	state of, action of	reaction, completion
-ish	rather, a bit	plumpish, yellowish
-ism	set of beliefs	Marxism, socialism
-ism	prejudice	racism, sexism
-ist	believer	Marxist, socialist
-ist	prejudiced person	racist, sexist
-itis	inflamed body part	tonsillitis, diverticulitis
-ition	state of, action of	composition, juxtaposition
-ity	state of, condition of	acidity, sexuality
-ive	tending to	depressive, selective
-ize, -ise	cause to become	privatize, fictionalize
-kin	small	lambkin, wolfkin
-less	without	tasteless, strapless
-like	similar to	apelike, wifelike
-ling	small	pigling, duckling
-logy, -ology	study of, science of	biology, geology
-ly	in this way	quickly, merrily
-ment	state of, action of	management, agreement
-meter	measuring device	thermometer, speedometer
-metry	measuring	geometry, audiometry
-ness	state of, quality of	brightness, gentleness
-nik	person involved in	beatnik, refusenik
-nomy	study or rules of	astronomy, taxonomy
-onym, -nym	word, name	synonym, eponym
-pathy	disease	adenopathy, sociopathy
-ship	state of, condition of	friendship, dictatorship
-sion	state of, action of	confusion, inclusion

Word	Meaning	Examples
-some	tending to	quarrelsome, cuddlesome
-tion	state of, action of	co-operation, navigation
-tomy, -ectomy	surgery upon	colostomy, appendectomy
-vore	one who feeds on	herbivore, carnivore
-vorous	feeding on	omnivorous, vermivorous
-ware	manufactured material	silverware, ironware
-ways	in the direction of	sideways, edgeways
-wise	in the manner of	clockwise, crabwise
-wise	regarding	dietwise, workwise
-wright	maker of	shipwright, wheelwright
-y	full of, similar to	creamy, doggy

Root words

Word	Meaning	Examples
aero	air	aeroplane, anaerobe
ambi	both	ambidextrous, ambiguous
anthrop	human	anthropology, misanthropic
aqua	water	aquarium, subaqua

Insight

Aqua is the Latin word meaning 'water'. The root word hydro is the Greek equivalent. The Greek for water is *hudor*. Both root words have been used extensively to create words that are current in English.

audi	hear	audience, inaudible
auto	self	autobiography, autonomous
bio	life, living	biology, antibiotic
cede	yield	cede, precede
cred	believe	credible, discredit
crypt	hidden	cryptic, encryption

(Contd)

Word	Meaning	Examples
cycl	circle, wheel	cyclone, recycle
duo	two	duet, duotone
graph	writing	graphite, autograph
gyn	woman	gynaecology, androgynous
hydro	water	hydrogen, dehydrate
lingua	tongue, language	linguistic, bilingual
mort	death	mortal, amortize
nova	new	novel, supernova
ped	foot	pedicure, quadruped
phil	love	philosophy, Francophile
phob	hatred, fear	phobia, xenophobe
phon	sound	phonetic, microphone
photo	light	photograph, telephoto
port	carry	portable, export
prim	first	primary, primitive
psych	the mind	psychology, psyche
scope	examine	telescope, periscope
scribe	write	scribble, transcribe
theo	God, god	theology, polytheism
tox	poison	toxic, intoxicate
tract	pulling	tractor, subtract
vac	empty	vacuum, evacuate
verb	word	verbal, adverb
vert, vers	turning	vertebra, reverse
vis	see	visible, television

Exercise

The following words are combinations of prefixes, suffixes and root words that are all explained in this chapter. Can you work out what they mean?

- hydrophobia
- astrology
- omnivore
- polyhedron

- *neophilia*
- *bilingual*
- *aquiferous*
- *monotheism*
- *rhinoscope*
- *patricide*

Exercise

Can you find the prefixes, suffixes and root words for each of the words below and combine them to make an existing word?

- *self-writing*
- *study of animals*
- *pulling action*
- *related to blood*
- *device for measuring time*
- *government by women*
- *inflammation of the nose*
- *related to the name of the father*
- *disease of the mind*
- *related to having two feet*

EXERCISE

10-question diagnostic test

1 *Which prefix means 'similar'?*
2 *Which prefix means 'identical'?*
3 *Which prefix means 'straight'?*
4 *Which prefix means 'faulty'?*
5 *Which suffix means 'surgery upon'?*
6 *Which suffix means 'prejudice'?*
7 *Which suffix means 'in the direction of'?*
8 *Which root word means 'hidden'?*
9 *Which root word means 'death'?*
10 *Which root word means 'empty'?*

10 THINGS TO REMEMBER

1 *Prefixes, suffixes and root words are the building blocks of English.*

2 *A prefix is a letter or group of letters added to the beginning of a word to make a different word.*

3 *A suffix is a letter or group of letters added to the end of a word to make a different word.*

4 *An affix is a word for a prefix or a suffix.*

5 *A root word is a word from another language that can be used to make many other words.*

6 *A root word can be used at the beginning of, at the end of, or in the middle of a word.*

7 *Most root words are from Latin and Greek.*

8 *Some affixes have come into English very recently, such as* **cyber** *and* **e**.

9 *Understanding affixes and root words is a good way of improving your spelling.*

10 *Knowing the commonest root words also helps you to understand unfamiliar words.*

8

Which is which?

In this chapter you will learn:
- *how homophones can confuse and cause you to make spelling errors*
- *the definitions of commonly confused homophones*
- *how some English words can be spelt in more than one way and the correct spelling to use*
- *how pairs of English words sound so similar, it's easy to confuse them.*

Many of the problems that people have with English spelling come about because so many words sound the same as, or similar to, other words with different meanings.

Homophones

One of the most notable features of English is the large number of homophones it contains. A homophone is a word that sounds like another word but has a different spelling or a different meaning or, sometimes, both. The word homophone is from Greek *homos,* meaning 'same', and *phōnē*, meaning 'sound'. Some homophones are:

fritter *(to waste) and* **fritter** *(fried food) – same spelling, different meanings*

camomile *and* **chamomile** – *same meaning, different spellings*
flower *and* **flour** – *different meanings, different spellings*

These homophones can be confusing and are very often responsible for spelling mistakes, as the writer uses one word when it ought to be another. Below is a list of commonly confused homophones, with a short, easy-to-understand explanation of the meaning of each word.

air, heir
- ▶ **air** *is the gas we breathe: a breath of fresh air*
- ▶ *an* **heir** *is someone who inherits something: the heir to the throne*

altar, alter
- ▶ *an* **altar** *is a table in a church: there were candles on the altar*
- ▶ *to* **alter** *something is to change it: I asked him to alter the wording of the last paragraph*

ant, aunt
In some accents **ant** and **aunt** are homophones.

- ▶ *an* **ant** *is an insect*
- ▶ *your* **aunt** *is the sister of your father or mother, or the wife of your uncle*

ate, eight
- ▶ **ate** *is the past tense of the verb 'eat': he ate all his lunch*
- ▶ **eight** *is the number between seven and nine: our dog had eight puppies*

aural, oral
- ▶ **aural** *means 'relating to the sense of hearing': aural stimulus*
- ▶ **oral** *means 'relating to the mouth' or 'spoken': it was an oral examination*

aye, eye, I
- ▶ **aye** *means 'yes' or is a vote for something: we expect an aye from our MP*

- *an* **eye** *is the organ for seeing: a poke in the eye*
- **I** *is the pronoun used by the speaker or writer: I see you've had your hair cut*

bail, bale

- **bail** *is the money paid to get a prisoner out of jail for a time: who's going to pay bail for him?*
- *a* **bale** *is a large tight bundle of something: a bale of hay*

baited, bated

- **baited** *is the past tense and past participle of the verb 'bait': I baited the hook with a worm*
- *if you do something with* **bated breath**, *you do it anxiously: he waited with bated breath for the winner to be announced*

ball, bawl

- *a* **ball** *is a round toy: pass me the ball*
- *to* **bawl** *is to cry loudly: the baby started to bawl*
- *a* **bawl** *is a loud cry*

bare, bear

- **bare** *means 'naked' or 'uncovered': a bare torso*
- *to* **bare** *something is to uncover it*
- *a* **bear** *is a wild animal: lions and tigers and bears*
- *to* **bear** *something is to carry it or to endure it: he bears a heavy load; I can't bear that woman*

baron, barren

- *a* **baron** *is a nobleman: the barons of England*
- *land that is* **barren** *cannot produce crops: barren soil*
- *a* **barren** *woman cannot have a baby*

base, bass

- *the* **base** *is the bottom part of something: she looked closely at the base of the vase*
- *a* **bass** *is a singer with a low voice*
- **bass** *is also short for* **bass guitar**: *I play bass in the band*

baton, batten

▸ a **baton** *is a small wooden stick, for example that used by the conductor of an orchestra or in a relay race*
▸ a **batten** *is a piece of sawn timber*
▸ to **batten down** *the hatches is to prepare for bad weather or trouble*

bazaar, bizarre

▸ a **bazaar** *is a sale held to raise money for a cause: a church bazaar*
▸ *in the countries of the Middle East,* **bazaar** *is the word for the market*
▸ a **bizarre** *person behaves strangely: a bizarre man wearing a false beard and goggles*

be, bee

▸ **be** *is the verb meaning 'exist': to be or not to be*
▸ a **bee** *is an insect that buzzes and makes honey: I got stung by a bee*
▸ a **bee** *is also a group of people who get together to do something: a sewing bee*
▸ a **spelling bee** *is a spelling competition, especially one for children*

beach, beech

▸ a **beach** *is a stretch of sand next to the sea: a romantic walk on the beach*
▸ *something that is* **beached** *is on the shore: a beached whale*
▸ a **beech** *is a type of tree*

bean, been

▸ a **bean** *is an edible seed from a type of plant: a dish of runner beans and haricot beans*
▸ **been** *is the past participle of the verb 'be': where have you been all this time?*

beer, bier

▸ **beer** *is an alcoholic drink made from hops: a pint of beer and same sandwiches*

▶ a **bier** is a frame for carrying a dead body: they made a rough bier for their comrade's corpse.

blew, blue
▶ **blew** is the past tense of the verb 'blow': the referee blew the whistle
▶ **blue** is the colour of the sky on a sunny day: a light blue suit

boar, bore
▶ a **boar** is a male pig or a wild pig: a boar hunt
▶ a **bore** is someone or something that is not interesting in any way: I find weddings a total bore
▶ to **bore** a hole is to make a hole in something
▶ a **bore** is also a wave that rushes up some rivers: a tidal bore

bough, bow
▶ a **bough** is a branch of a tree: when the bough breaks the cradle will fall
▶ to **bow** is to bend your body as a greeting or mark of respect to someone: the men bowed to the queen
▶ the **bow** is the front part of a ship

boy, buoy
▶ a **boy** is a male child: they have two girls and one boy
▶ a **buoy** is a floating object that is used to guide ships: don't swim out beyond the buoy

brake, break
▶ a **brake** is the mechanism that stops or slows down a vehicle: don't forget to put the brake on when you park
▶ when you **brake**, you apply the brakes to stop or slow down
▶ to **break** is to fall apart or to make something fall apart: I saw him break the window
▶ a **break** in something is a pause: we'll wait for a break in the rain and then we'll run for it

bread, bred
▶ **bread** is food made from flour that has been mixed and baked: wholemeal bread

- ▶ **bred** *is the past tense and past participle of the verb 'breed':* *these sheep have been bred for their wool*

bridal, bridle
- ▶ **bridal** *is related to a bride or a wedding: a bridal gown*
- ▶ *a* **bridle** *is a harness put on a horse's head*
- ▶ *to* **bridle** *is to react indignantly to something that annoys you*

broach, brooch
- ▶ *to* **broach** *a subject is to begin talking about it: she was reluctant to broach the subject of Christmas Day*
- ▶ *a* **brooch** *is a piece of jewellery that is pinned on to clothes: a diamond brooch*

but, butt
- ▶ **but** *is a conjunction that shows a contrast: I like my colleagues but I hate my boss.*
- ▶ *a* **butt** *is a large barrel, the heavy end of a rifle, and the finished end of a cigarette*
- ▶ **butt** *is also an American slang word for buttocks*
- ▶ *if you* **butt** *something, you hit it with your head*
- ▶ *to* **butt in** *is to interrupt a conversation: I warned her not to butt in when I was on the phone*

buy, by, bye
- ▶ *to* **buy** *something is to get it in exchange for money: I would love to buy a new car*
- ▶ *a* **buy** *is a purchase: that bag was a really good buy*
- ▶ **by** *is an adverb and preposition used to indicate various ideas including nearness, action and passing movement: a house by the sea; we sat on a bench watching people stroll by; a painting by Monet*
- ▶ **bye** *is another word for goodbye: bye, losers!*
- ▶ *a* **bye** *is also a kind of run scored in cricket*

callous, callus
- ▶ *someone* **callous** *is cruel and hardhearted*
- ▶ *a* **callus** *is a piece of thick or hard skin*

cannon, canon

- ▶ a **cannon** is a large gun on wheels
- ▶ a **canon** is a member of the clergy
- ▶ a **canon** is also an established list: the canon of English literature

canvas, canvass

- ▶ **canvas** is a type of strong cloth used for sails and tents, and also for painting on: a night under canvas
- ▶ to **canvass** is to go about trying to get support for something, especially in an election: there are plans to canvass the whole constituency

carat, caret, carrot

- ▶ a **carat** is a measurement for ranking gold and gemstones: nine-carat gold
- ▶ a **caret** is a symbol written to show that something should be inserted in a piece of text
- ▶ a **carrot** is an orange root vegetable

cell, sell

- ▶ a **cell** is a small room for a prisoner in jail: he spends 23 hours a day in his cell
- ▶ a **cell** is also a biology word for the smallest unit of any living thing
- ▶ the American term for mobile phone is **cell phone**. Just as British people shorten **mobile phone** to **mobile**, Americans often shorten **cell phone** to **cell**: call me on my cell and let me know
- ▶ to **sell** something is to hand it over for money: I would like to sell this house and move to the country

censer, censor

- ▶ a **censer** is a container used for burning incense in a church
- ▶ a **censor** is a person whose job is to examine books and films and decide whether they should be made public

cent, scent, sent

- ▶ a **cent** is a coin worth one hundredth of an American dollar and also one hundredth of a euro: a ten-cent piece

- ▶ a **scent** is a smell: *the scent of lavender*
- ▶ to **scent** is to discover by smell or to give a pleasant smell to: *these dogs can scent the fox straight away*
- ▶ **sent** is the past tense and past participle of the verb 'send': *I sent him a birthday card but it never arrived*

cereal, serial

- ▶ **cereal** is grain that is used as food: *cereal crops*
- ▶ **cereal** is also a breakfast food made from grain: *I'll just have cereal and toast, thanks*
- ▶ a **serial** is a story that is shown on TV or broadcast on the radio in instalments: *a television serial adapted from the best-selling novel*

check, cheque

- ▶ to **check** something is to make sure it is correct or is working properly: *let me check that email before you send it*
- ▶ **check** also means 'to stop or hold back'
- ▶ a **check** is a test to see something is correct or working properly: *a health check*
- ▶ a **check** is also a square or a pattern of squares
- ▶ a **cheque** is a piece of paper that allows the bank to pay money from one person to another: *a cheque for two thousand pounds*

chord, cord

- ▶ a **chord** is a musical sound made when you play several notes together: *I can only play two chords on the guitar*
- ▶ **chord** is in mathematics a straight line that joins any two places on a curve
- ▶ a **cord** is a thin rope or thick strand of something: *she keeps her glasses on a cord round her neck*
- ▶ in anatomy, a **cord** is a long flexible piece of the body: *spinal cord; vocal cords; umbilical cord*
- ▶ **cords** are trousers made from a ribbed cotton material called corduroy

cite, sight, site

▶ to **cite** *something is to mention it as an example or proof: more than a dozen former employees were willing to cite occurrences of bullying*

▶ to **cite** *is also to summon a person to appear in court*

▶ **sight** *is the ability to see: amazingly, he regained his sight in his twenties*

▶ a **sight** *is something that is worth seeing: the sights of New York*

▶ to **sight** *is to get a view of: the crew had been sailing for a week when they sighted land*

▶ a **site** *is a place where a building is to be placed: the site of the new supermarket*

▶ to **site** *something is to choose a place for it to be built or placed: a plan to site a mobile phone mast on the roof of the rugby club*

▶ a **site** *is a website on the internet: a great site for second-hand clothes*

coarse, course

▶ *something* **coarse** *has a rough surface: coarse sand*

▶ **coarse** *also means 'vulgar': a coarse expression*

▶ **coarse fishing** *is fishing for freshwater fish other than salmon*

▶ a **course** *is a path along which someone or something moves: the course of the river*

▶ a **course** *is a part of a meal: two courses for £10*

▶ a **course** *is also a number of lessons or lectures on a subject: a business course*

complement, compliment

▶ a **complement** *is something that goes well with another thing: this wine is the perfect complement to beef*

▶ to **complement** *is to go well with: choose colours that complement your skin tone*

▶ to **complement** *is also to complete or add to: dietary advice to complement the medical treatment*

▶ to **compliment** *someone is to say something flattering about them: he made sure to compliment her on the success of her book*

▶ a **compliment** *is a flattering comment*

complementary, complimentary

- ▶ *something* **complementary** *goes well with another thing:* complementary colours
- ▶ **complementary medicine** *is the name used for treatments such as homeopathy and acupuncture*
- ▶ *a* **complimentary** *comment is flattering: he was very complimentary about your work*
- ▶ **complimentary** *can also mean 'given for free': complimentary tickets; a complimentary bottle of wine*

council, counsel

- ▶ *a* **council** *is a group of people who have been elected to run something: the local council*
- ▶ *the* **Privy Council** *is the group of people who advise the king or queen*
- ▶ **counsel** *is advice: wise counsel*
- ▶ **counsel** *is a formal word for a lawyer or a group of lawyers working together: defence counsel*
- ▶ *to* **counsel** *is to offer advice: most experts would counsel caution in these circumstances*

councillor, counsellor

- ▶ *a* **councillor** *is a member of a council: many local councillors back the proposals*
- ▶ *a* **counsellor** *is someone who offers advice: a marriage counsellor*
- ▶ *a* **Privy Counsellor** *is a member of the Privy Council*

creak, creek

- ▶ *to* **creak** *is to make an unpleasant grating sound: I heard the door creak open overhead*
- ▶ *a* **creak** *is an unpleasant grating sound: the creak of footsteps on the stairs*
- ▶ *a* **creek** *is either a small bay on the sea coast or a short river: up the creek without a paddle*

curb, kerb

- ▶ *to* **curb** *is to hold back or restrain: to curb public spending*
- ▶ *a* **curb** *is a restraint: a curb on inflation*
- ▶ *the* **kerb** *is the edge of the pavement*

currant, current

▶ a **currant** *is a small black raisin: a cake with currants and sultanas*

▶ a **current** *is a stream of water, air or electrical power that is moving in one direction: the body was carried out to sea by the current; warm currents of air*

▶ *something that is* **current** *is related to the present time: the current government*

cygnet, signet

▶ a **cygnet** *is a young swan*

▶ a **signet** *is a small seal with somebody's initials on it*

cymbal, symbol

▶ a **cymbal** *is a brass musical instrument shaped like a plate, which is hit against another cymbal to make a noise*

▶ a **symbol** *is something that represents another thing: the winged lion is the symbol of Venice*

▶ a **symbol** *is also a printed character used to stand in for something else: + is the symbol for plus*

dear, deer

▶ *something* **dear** *costs a lot of money: the house is too dear for us*

▶ *someone* **dear** *is much loved: a dear friend from school*

▶ a **dear** *is a person you love or who is lovable: your grandfather is a dear*

▶ a **deer** *is an animal like the reindeer or elk, the male of which has antlers*

dependant, dependent

▶ a **dependant** *is a person who depends on another person for money to live on: children or other dependants*

▶ *someone who is* **dependent** *relies or depends on someone or something: a dependent relative; dependent on alcohol*

desert, dessert

▶ *to* **desert** *is to run away from or abandon: he was accused of encouraging other soldiers to desert; floods forced them to desert their village*

- ▶ a **desert** *is a piece of dry country with little or no rainfall: the Gobi Desert*
- ▶ a **dessert** *is the final course of a meal which can be sweets or fruit: the dessert menu*

discreet, discrete
- ▶ *someone* **discreet** *is careful about what they say: a very discreet conversation*
- ▶ **discrete** *means 'separate or distinct': a series of discrete steps*

draft, draught
- ▶ a **draft** *is a rough version of something that is being worked on: this is not the final report, it's only a draft*
- ▶ a **draught** *is a current of air: I'm sitting in a draught here*
- ▶ **draught beer** *is stored in a barrel rather than in individual bottles*
- ▶ **draughts** *is a game similar to chess played on a board*
- ▶ a **draughtsman** *or* **draughtswoman** *is employed to draw plans*

dual, duel, jewel
- ▶ **dual** *means 'consisting of two': dual carriageway; dual-purpose*
- ▶ a **duel** *is a formal fight between two people, either with guns or swords*
- ▶ *to* **duel** *is to fight in a duel*
- ▶ a **jewel** *is a precious stone*
- ▶ a **jewel** *is also a person or a thing that is highly valued: the jewel in the company's chain of shops*

eerie, eyrie
- ▶ *something* **eerie** *is frightening because it is unknown: an eerie voice*
- ▶ *an* **eyrie** *is an eagle's nest*

ewe, yew, you
- ▶ a **ewe** *is a female sheep*
- ▶ a **yew** *is a kind of tree with red berries*
- ▶ **you** *is the pronoun for the person being spoken to or written to: you are sitting in my seat; have you seen my dog?*

faint, feint

- ▶ to **faint** *is to collapse into unconsciousness*
- ▶ *if you feel* **faint**, *you are about to lose consciousness*
- ▶ **faint** *also means 'lacking in strength or brightness': the faint sound of music; faint colours*
- ▶ *a* **faint** *is an episode of fainting: he fell down in a faint*
- ▶ *a* **feint** *is an act of pretence which is intended to put someone off their guard: he turned and made a feint towards the door*
- ▶ to **feint** *is to make an act of pretence like this*
- ▶ **feint** *paper has pale lines printed on it: a narrow feint*

fair, fare, fayre

- ▶ **fair** *hair is light in colour*
- ▶ **fair** *weather is clear and dry*
- ▶ *something that is* **fair** *is unbiased and just: a fair decision*
- ▶ *if something is* **fair**, *it is good enough but not excellent*
- ▶ *a* **fair** *is a large market: a cattle fair*
- ▶ *a* **fair** *is also an exhibition of different producers of a particular thing: the Frankfurt Book Fair*
- ▶ *a* **fair** *is a travelling collection of rides and sideshows such as merry-go-rounds and dodgems*
- ▶ *the* **fare** *is the price of a journey: how much is the fare to Glasgow Central?*
- ▶ **fare** *is also a word for food: festive fare*
- ▶ *some people use* **fayre** *as a deliberately old-fashioned word for both* **fair** *and* **fare**, *but it is probably best to avoid it*

faun, fawn

- ▶ *a* **faun** *is an imaginary creature with the body of a man and the legs of a goat*
- ▶ *a* **fawn** *is a young deer*
- ▶ **fawn** *is also a light yellowish-brown colour: fawn trousers*
- ▶ to **fawn on** *someone is to flatter them in an embarrassingly grovelling way: I hate the way you fawn over that woman*

faze, phase

- ▶ to **faze** *is to disturb or worry: Murray doesn't let all the attention faze him*

- ▸ a **phase** is a stage in a process: *the first phase of my plan for world domination*
- ▸ to **phase in** is to introduce something in stages
- ▸ to **phase out** is to remove something in stages

feat, feet
- ▸ a **feat** is an action that needs some effort to achieve: *an amazing feat of engineering*
- ▸ **feet** is the plural of 'foot': *the whole world is at his feet; a wall ten feet tall*

flair, flare
- ▸ a **flair** is a talent or skill: *a flair for decorating*
- ▸ to do something with **flair** is to do it in a stylish way: *she dresses with enormous flair*
- ▸ a **flare** is a bright light used as a signal: *an enemy flare lit up the sky*
- ▸ to **flare** is to burn more brightly
- ▸ to **flare** or **flare up** is to begin: *police fear trouble will flare when night comes*
- ▸ **flares** are trousers which get very wide below the knee

flea, flee
- ▸ a **flea** is a small biting insect that can jump very high
- ▸ to **flee** is to run away from danger: *they had to flee the country after receiving death threats*

flour, flower
- ▸ **flour** is finely ground wheat used for making bread and cakes: *wholemeal flour*
- ▸ a **flower** is the part of a plant from which the fruit or seeds grow: *a garden full of flowers*

floury, flowery
- ▸ something **floury** is covered with flour: *floury rolls*
- ▸ something **flowery** is full of or decorated with flowers: *flowery curtains*
- ▸ **flowery** language is fancy and a bit overdone

forth, fourth

▶ **forth** *means 'forward': he paced back and forth in
   the hallway*
▶ *the Scottish river with the famous railway bridge is the
   River* **Forth**
▶ *something that is* **fourth** *comes after the first three things in
   a series: the fourth episode*
▶ *a* **fourth** *of something is a quarter of it*

foul, fowl

▶ *something* **foul** *smells or tastes very bad: foul coffee*
▶ **foul** *language is full of swearing*
▶ *a* **foul** *in a game is an act of breaking the rules*
▶ *if you* **foul**, *you break the rules of a game*
▶ *if a dog* **fouls**, *it drops faeces on the ground*
▶ *a* **fowl** *is a bird such as a chicken*

freeze, frieze

▶ *to* **freeze** *is to turn into ice*
▶ *to* **freeze** *food is to make it very cold in order to make it last
   longer: is it safe to freeze bacon?*
▶ *if you* **freeze**, *you go stiff with cold or fear: I was scared I
   would freeze in the interview*
▶ *a* **frieze** *is a part of a wall that is decorated: Roman friezes*

gamble, gambol

▶ *to* **gamble** *is to risk money on the result of a game or race:
   he promised his father he would never gamble*
▶ *a* **gamble** *is a risk or a bet on a particular result: it would
   be a big gamble to leave your job without having another
   one to go to*
▶ *to* **gambol** *is to jump about playfully: lambs could gambol
   in the grassy fields*

gait, gate

▶ *someone's* **gait** *is the way they walk: a hurried gait*
▶ *a* **gate** *is a door across an opening: the garden gate; the
   school gate*

gild, guild

▶ to **gild** is to cover with beaten gold

▶ to **gild the lily** is to try to improve something that is already excellent: *to add more chocolate to this cake would be to gild the lily, I think*

▶ a **guild** is a group of people who work together in a particular business or who socialize together: *the Screenwriters' Guild; the Women's Guild*

gilt, guilt

▶ **gilt** is beaten gold that is used in gilding

▶ something that is **gilt** is either covered with thinly beaten gold or is gold in colour: *a gilt mirror*

▶ **guilt** is a feeling of shame at having done something wrong

▶ **guilt** is also blame for doing something wrong: *his guilt has never been in doubt*

gorilla, guerrilla

▶ a **gorilla** is a kind of large ape: *mountain gorillas*

▶ a **guerrilla** is a fighter who makes sudden attacks on the enemy without fighting out in the open

grate, great

▶ to **grate** food is to rub it against something rough in order to break it into small pieces: *grate two large carrots*

▶ a **grate** is also a metal frame for holding a fire

▶ something **great** is very large, very important, very talented or very good: *a great castle; a great leader; a great party*

grisly, grizzly

▶ something **grisly** is nasty and horrible: *a grisly murder*

▶ a **grizzly** or **grizzly bear** is a large North American bear

groan, grown

▶ to **groan** is to moan in pain or distress

▶ a **groan** is the sound of a groan: *she gave a groan as she tried to stand up*

▶ **grown** *is the past participle of the verb 'grow': that hedge has grown a foot since last year*

hair, hare
▶ *a* **hair** *is a thread-like growth on the skin of an animal and on the head of a person: I prefer dogs with smooth hair; I need to get my hair cut before the wedding*
▶ *a* **hare** *is an animal rather like a large rabbit, which can run very fast*

hall, haul
▶ *a* **hall** *is a passage at the entrance to a house: she made me stand in the hall while she got her coat on*
▶ *a* **hall** *is also a large public room: a bingo hall*
▶ *a* **haul** *is a strong pull at something: a haul on the rope*
▶ *a* **haul** *is also a difficult job: a long haul*
▶ *to* **haul** *is to pull hard: they had to haul him out of the water*

hangar, hanger
▶ *a* **hangar** *is a large shed for aeroplanes*
▶ *a* **hanger** *is a frame for hanging clothes on*

hart, heart
▶ *a* **hart** *is a male deer*
▶ *the* **heart** *is the organ that pumps blood around the body: heart surgery*

hay, hey
▶ **hay** *is grass that has been dried and cut and is fed to cattle*
▶ **hey** *is said to attract a person's attention*

heal, heel, he'll
▶ *to* **heal** *is make or become healthy: stop picking that or it will never heal*
▶ *the* **heel** *is the back part of the foot*
▶ **he'll** *is short for 'he will' or 'he shall': no doubt he'll be late as usual*

heard, herd

▶ **heard** *is the past tense and past participle of the verb 'hear': I heard you were getting married; I've heard that song before*

▶ *a* **herd** *is a group of animals of one kind: a herd of wildebeest*

heroin, heroine

▶ **heroin** *is a strong illegal drug made from poppies: he is a heroin addict*

▶ *a* **heroine** *is a woman who has done something admirable, especially something brave: a heroine of World War II*

▶ *the* **heroine** *of a story or film is the chief female character in it: the heroine of 'Pride and Prejudice'*

him, hymn

▶ **him** *is a pronoun that refers to a male person who has already been spoken about: we saw him in the supermarket*

▶ *a* **hymn** *is a song praising God*

hoard, horde

▶ *a* **hoard** *is a hidden store of something, especially treasure or food: an Anglo-Saxon hoard*

▶ *to* **hoard** *is to store up secretly*

▶ *a* **horde** *is a large crowd or group: two teachers surrounded by a horde of children*

holey, holy, wholly

▶ *something* **holey** *is full of holes: tattered shirts and holey jumpers*

▶ *something* **holy** *is religious or for religious use: the holy book of Islam*

▶ **wholly** *is completely: the award is wholly deserved*

hour, our

▶ *an* **hour** *is a measurement of time, sixty minutes in length: the journey takes an hour*

▶ **our** *is a pronoun that means 'belonging to us': our school has been closed for a week now*

idle, idol

- ▶ to be **idle** *is to be lazy or not working: the idle rich; the factories are idle*
- ▶ an **idol** *is an image that is worshipped as a god*
- ▶ an **idol** *is also someone who is much admired: Hollywood idol George Clooney*

in, inn

- ▶ **in** *is a preposition that shows position in space or time: in the cupboard; in the last century*
- ▶ *if something is* **in**, *it is fashionable: the in place to eat this month*
- ▶ an **inn** *is a pub or small hotel in the country*

it's, its

- ▶ **it's** *is short for 'it is' or 'it has': it's very windy tonight; it's been like that all week*
- ▶ **its** *is the pronoun that indicates 'belonging to it': the horse broke its leg; put the camera back in its case; the film takes its title from the lead character*

key, quay

- ▶ a **key** *is an object that is used to lock and unlock a door*
- ▶ a **key** *is a button on a computer keyboard*
- ▶ *something* **key** *is very important or essential: romance is the key ingredient for this book*
- ▶ a **quay** *is a landing place for loading and unloading boats: a ferry quay*

knave, nave

- ▶ a **knave** *is the jack in playing cards*
- ▶ a **knave** *is also an old-fashioned word for a rogue*
- ▶ *the* **nave** *is the main part of a church*

knead, need

- ▶ to **knead** *dough is to press it with the fingers*
- ▶ to **need** *something is to be without it or to require it: we need money; I need onions for the soup*

knew, new

- ▶ **knew** *is the past tense of the verb 'know': I knew you wouldn't let me down*
- ▶ *something* **new** *has not been seen or known before: a new film from the Coen Brothers; a new shoe shop*
- ▶ **new** *is not used or worn: new shoes; a new toothbrush*

knot, not

- ▶ *a* **knot** *is a lump made by tying a piece of string*
- ▶ *a* **knot** *is also a bump on a piece of wood where a branch once grew*
- ▶ *a* **knot** *is a measure of speed for ships*
- ▶ *if you* **knot** *something, you tie it in a knot: don't forget to knot your thread before you start sewing*
- ▶ **not** *is an adverb that expresses refusal or denial: I am not going to her party; he has not been on holiday*

lain, lane

- ▶ **lain** *is the past participle of the verb 'lie': the old man had lain on the floor for two days*
- ▶ *a* **lane** *is a narrow street: Pudding Lane*
- ▶ *a* **lane** *is one of the parts that a road is divided into: the inside lane*

leach, leech

- ▶ *to* **leach** *is to let liquid slowly leak out of something: pesticides can leach into rivers and streams*
- ▶ *a* **leech** *is a kind of blood-sucking worm*

lead, led

- ▶ **lead** *is a soft metal*
- ▶ *the* **lead** *of a pencil is the bit that writes (although it is actually graphite, not lead)*
- ▶ **led** *is the past tense and past participle of the verb 'lead': the captains led the teams out on to the pitch; she claims she has been led astray*

leak, leek

- ▶ a **leak** is a hole through which liquid or gas can escape
- ▶ a **leak** is also an escape of liquid or gas: *the explosion was caused by a gas leak*
- ▶ if gas or liquid **leaks**, it escapes
- ▶ a **leek** is a green and white vegetable related to the onion

lessen, lesson

- ▶ to **lessen** is to make smaller: *we need to lessen public debt*
- ▶ a **lesson** is something that is learnt or taught: *a French lesson*

liar, lyre

- ▶ a **liar** is someone who tells lies: *liar, liar, pants on fire!*
- ▶ a **lyre** is an old musical instrument similar to a harp

licence, license

- ▶ a **licence** is a document that gives permission to do something: *a driving licence*
- ▶ to **license** something is to allow it: *the government is unwilling to license this drug at the present time*
- ▶ **licence** is the noun and **license** is the verb

lightening, lightning

- ▶ **lightening** is the present participle of the verb 'lighten': *the sky was lightening as daybreak approached*
- ▶ **lightening** is also an occurrence of becoming lighter or brighter
- ▶ **lightning** is a flash of electricity in the clouds often seen in thunder storms

loan, lone

- ▶ a **loan** is something that has been lent: *a loan from my parents*
- ▶ to **loan** something is to lend it: *banks are not keen to loan money just now*
- ▶ **lone** means 'alone': *a lone rider was coming across the field*

loot, lute

- **loot** *is something that has been stolen: the gang made off with their loot before the police could get there*
- *to* **loot** *is to carry off goods illegally: mobs began to loot the empty shops*
- *a* **lute** *is an old-fashioned stringed musical instrument that is played by plucking*

made, maid

- **made** *is the past tense and past participle of the verb 'make': we made a cake for your birthday; I think you have made a mistake*
- *a* **maid** *is a female servant: a ladies' maid*
- *a* **maid** *is also an old-fashioned name for an unmarried woman*

mail, male

- **mail** *is letters and parcels carried by post*
- **mail** *is also email*
- *to* **mail** *is to send by post or to email*
- **mail** *is body armour made of steel rings or plates*
- *a* **male** *is a member of the sex that is able to father children: an alpha male*

main, mane

- **main** *means 'most important': she is the main reason I left*
- *the* **main** *is also an old-fashioned word for ocean: the Spanish Main*
- *a* **mane** *is the long thick hair on the head and neck of a horse or male lion*

maize, maze

- **maize** *is a type of corn grown for food*
- *a* **maze** *is a series of winding paths designed to make it difficult to find the way out: Hampton Court Maze*

marshal, martial

- *a* **marshal** *is an officer high up in the army or air force*
- *to* **marshal** *troops is to arrange them according to plan*

- ▶ **martial** *means 'relating to war or fighting': martial law; martial music*
- ▶ **martial arts** *are methods of fighting such as judo and karate*

meat, meet, mete
- ▶ **meat** *is the flesh of an animal used as food*
- ▶ *to* **meet** *is to come face to face with or get to know: where did you meet your wife?*
- ▶ *to* **mete out** *is to deal out: some people believe it is for God to mete out punishment, not man*

medal, meddle
- ▶ *a* **medal** *is a metal disc often given as a prize: he won three gold medals at the Olympics*
- ▶ *to* **medal** *is to win a medal: no one expected her to medal at these games*
- ▶ *to* **meddle** *is to interfere in things that are not your concern: his friends keep trying to meddle in his love life*

metal, mettle
- ▶ *a* **metal** *is a substance that can conduct heat and electricity*
- ▶ *something* **metal** *is made of metal: a metal box*
- ▶ **mettle** *is an old-fashioned word for courage: this match will really test their mettle*

meter, metre
- ▶ *a* **meter** *is an instrument for measuring something: an electricity meter*
- ▶ *a* **metre** *is a unit of length*
- ▶ *in poetry,* **metre** *is the arrangement of words in a regular rhythm*

might, mite
- ▶ **might** *is the past tense of the verb 'may': he might have left already*
- ▶ **might** *is power or strength: the military might of the USA*
- ▶ *a* **mite** *is a small child: poor little mite*
- ▶ *a* **mite** *is also a kind of very small spider: red spider mite*

▶ a mite *means 'rather': she seems a mite embarrassed about the fuss*

miner, minor, myna, mynah
▶ *a* miner *is someone who digs coal out of a mine*
▶ *a* minor *is someone who is not yet legally an adult*
▶ *something* minor *is not very big or important: a minor difficulty*

In some accents myna and mynah are homophones of miner and minor.

▶ *a* myna *or* mynah *is a type of bird that can imitate human speech*

moose, mousse
▶ *a* moose *is a large animal similar to a deer*
▶ *a* mousse *is a light food made with eggs and cream: chocolate mousse; salmon mousse*
▶ mousse *is also a foamy substance that is used for styling the hair*

mucus, mucous
▶ mucus *is the slimy fluid that comes out of the nose*
▶ *if something is* mucous, *it is covered with or similar to mucus*
▶ *a* mucous *membrane is a lining of a cavity in the body that produces mucus*

muscle, mussel
▶ *a* muscle *is a part of the body that causes movement: stomach muscles*
▶ *a* mussel *is a kind of edible shellfish*

naught, nought
▶ naught *is an old-fashioned word for nothing: our plans have come to naught*
▶ nought *is zero, that is the figure* o: *a million is* 1 *followed by* 6 *noughts*
▶ noughts and crosses *is a game played by two players on a grid of nine squares*

naval, navel

- **naval** *means 'relating to the navy': naval history*
- *the* **navel** *is the belly button*
- *a* **navel** *or* **navel orange** *is a type of sweet orange*

pail, pale

- *a* **pail** *is a bucket*
- *a* **pale** *is a wooden stake in a fence*
- *something* **pale** *is light in colour: a pale sky*
- *to* **pale** *is to become pale*

pain, pane

- *a* **pain** *is a feeling of discomfort caused by hurt to the body or mind*
- *to* **pain** *someone is to distress them: you pain me when you say things like that*
- *a* **pane** *is a sheet of glass*

pair, pare, pear

- *a* **pair** *is a set of two things: a pair of shoes*
- *to* **pair** *is to join up to become two: the teacher asked the class to pair up*
- *to* **pare** *is to cut the outer edge or surface from: pare the rind from two lemons*
- *to* **pare** *is also to make smaller: we have been trying to pare costs all year*
- *a* **pear** *is a type of fruit with juicy white flesh*

palate, palette, pallet

- *the* **palate** *is the roof of the mouth*
- *a* **palette** *is the board on which an artist mixes paint*
- *a* **pallet** *is a straw bed or mattress*
- *a* **pallet** *is also a platform used for stacking goods*

passed, past

- **passed** *is the past tense and past participle of the verb 'pass': we passed on the staircase; I told him I had passed my driving test years ago*

- ▶ the **past** is time that has gone by
- ▶ **past** means 'from an earlier time' and 'finished': past insults; the opportunity to apologize is past
- ▶ **past** is a preposition meaning 'after' and 'beyond': past noon; I drove past the garage and then stopped
- ▶ **past** also means 'by': did I see you walking past my house this morning?

pea, pee

- ▶ a **pea** is a climbing plant that produces green edible seeds in pods
- ▶ **pee** is an informal word for urine, urinate and urination: your dog just had a pee on my rug

peace, piece

- ▶ **peace** is quietness and calm: I need peace to work
- ▶ **peace** is also the absence of war: there has been peace now for many years
- ▶ a **piece** is a part or portion of something: a piece of bread; a piece of marble

peak, peek, pique

- ▶ the **peak** of a mountain or hill is the highest part
- ▶ to **peak** is to reach the highest point: we expect unemployment to peak towards the end of next year
- ▶ to **peek** is to glance at something secretly
- ▶ a **peek** is a secret glance: I had a quick peek in his office when he was at lunch
- ▶ **pique** is anger caused by disappointment or resentment: a fit of pique
- ▶ to **pique** is to hurt someone's pride
- ▶ to **pique** interest or curiosity in something is to arouse it: they hope this story will pique the media's interest

peal, peel

- ▶ a **peal** is a set of bells
- ▶ a **peal** is also a series of loud sounds: a peal of laughter
- ▶ to **peal** bells is to ring them loudly

- ▶ *to* **peel** *is to strip the outer covering or skin of: peel me a grape*
- ▶ *when skin or paint* **peels**, *it comes off in small flakes*
- ▶ *a* **peel** *is the skin or rind of something: apple peel*

pedal, peddle

- ▶ *a* **pedal** *is a lever that is worked by the foot: bicycle pedal*
- ▶ *to* **pedal** *is to work the pedals of something*
- ▶ *to* **peddle** *is to travel from house to house selling something: to peddle double glazing*
- ▶ *to* **peddle** *is also to sell or promote something unpleasant or dishonest: the footballer claims the newspaper has been peddling lies about his private life*

peer, pier

- ▶ *a* **peer** *is a person's equal in ability, age or status: a jury of one's peers*
- ▶ *a* **peer** *is also a nobleman: a peer of the realm*
- ▶ *to* **peer** *is to look with half-closed eyes: I had to peer to read the writing at the bottom of the page*
- ▶ *a* **pier** *is a platform that reaches from the shore into the sea as a landing place for ships*

pidgin, pigeon

- ▶ *a* **pidgin** *is a simplified version of a language*
- ▶ *a* **pigeon** *is a type of bird*

place, plaice

- ▶ *a* **place** *is any particular physical location: a good place to meet; the pain is now in a different place*
- ▶ *to* **place** *is to put in a particular location*
- ▶ *a* **plaice** *is a type of edible fish*

Insight

Both these words come ultimately from the same Greek word, *platus* meaning 'broad' or 'flat'. **Place** comes from the Latin *platea* meaning 'courtyard' (a broad flat place). **Plaice** comes from the Late Latin *platessa* meaning 'flatfish'. Both came into the English language in the thirteenth century.

plain, plane

- ▶ *something* **plain** *is simple or without decoration: a plain omelette; a plain carpet*
- ▶ **plain** *also means 'easy to understand': plain English*
- ▶ *a* **plain** *is a level stretch of land*
- ▶ *a* **plane** *is an aeroplane*
- ▶ *a* **plane** *is also a tool used for smoothing wood*
- ▶ *a* **plane** *is a type of tree with broad leaves*

pole, poll

- ▶ *a* **pole** *is a long thin piece of wood*
- ▶ *the* **Poles** *are the most northerly and the most southerly points on the Earth's surface*
- ▶ *a* **Pole** *is a person from Poland*
- ▶ *a* **poll** *is the counting of votes at an election, and also the total number of votes cast*
- ▶ *a* **poll** *or* **opinion poll** *is a test of public opinion in which a representative sample of people is asked what they think about something*

pore, pour, paw

- ▶ *a* **pore** *is a tiny hole, especially one in the skin*
- ▶ *to* **pore over** *is to read very closely*
- ▶ *to* **pour** *is to flow in a stream: water began to pour through the ceiling; pour me a glass of wine*
- ▶ *to* **pour** *is to rain heavily*

In some accents **paw** is a homophone of **pore** and **pour**

- ▶ *a* **paw** *is an animal's foot*
- ▶ *if an animal* **paws***, it scrapes at something with one of its front paws*
- ▶ *to* **paw** *is to handle roughly or rudely*

practice, practise

- ▶ **practice** *is the repeated performance of something in order to improve it: singing practice*

- a **practice** *is the business of a professional person like a lawyer, doctor or veterinary surgeon*
- to **practise** *is to perform an activity repeatedly in order to improve*
- to **practise** *a profession is to work at it: to practise medicine*
- **practice** *is the noun and* **practise** *is the verb*

pray, prey
- to **pray** *is to speak to God*
- to **pray** *is also to beg*
- **prey** *is an animal hunted and killed by other animals for food*
- to **prey** on *is to kill and eat: barn owls prey on small mammals*
- to **prey** on *is also to select as a victim: conmen who prey on pensioners*

principal, principle
- **principal** *means 'most important': the country's principal source of income*
- the **principal** *is the head of a school or university*
- a **principle** *is a general truth or law: a fundamental principle of democracy*
- a person's **principles** *are their own personal rules of behaviour, according to their sense of right and wrong*

prise, prize
- to **prise** *is to force open: the burglar tried to prise the door off the safe*
- a **prize** *is a reward given for an achievement*
- to **prize** *is to value highly: I will prize this gift for the rest of my life*

profit, prophet
- a **profit** *is money made from selling something*
- to **profit** *is to benefit from something: convicted criminals are not allowed to profit from their crimes*
- a **prophet** *is someone who claims to be able to tell what will happen in the future*

rain, reign, rein

▶ **rain** *is water falling from the sky*
▶ *if it* **rains,** *water falls from the sky: the forecast says it will rain later today*
▶ *to* **reign** *is to rule a country*
▶ *a* **reign** *is the time when someone rules a place: the reign of Queen Victoria*
▶ *a* **rein** *is a strap used to guide a horse*
▶ *to* **rein** *is to control: the government wants to rein public spending*

raise, raze

▶ *to* **raise** *is to lift up or make higher or greater: we are going to have to raise the floorboards; I got them to raise my salary*
▶ *to* **raze** *is to knock down or destroy: Cromwell threatened to raze the town to the ground*

rap, wrap

▶ *a* **rap** *is a sharp knock: a rap at the front door*
▶ **rap** *is a kind of fast speaking done over a musical background: rap artists*
▶ *to* **rap** *is to perform this kind of speaking*
▶ *to* **wrap** *is to fold around or cover completely: wrap your fish in tinfoil; I still have to wrap all my Christmas presents*
▶ *a* **wrap** *is a kind of shawl*
▶ *a* **wrap** *is also a sandwich made with a tortilla: a chicken wrap*

read, reed

▶ *to* **read** *is to look at written words and understand them: I read the newspaper every day*
▶ *a* **reed** *is a type of tall stiff grass*
▶ *a* **reed** *is also a part of certain wind instruments*

read, red

▶ **read** *is the past tense and past participle of the verb 'read': I read that book last on holiday last year; have you ever read anything by Dan Brown?*
▶ **red** *is the colour of blood: red nails*

real, reel

▶ *if something is* **real***, it actually exists: are fairies real?*
▶ *something* **real** *is genuine and not fake: is that real fur?*
▶ *a* **reel** *is a cylinder for winding thread, string or wire: a cotton reel*
▶ *a* **reel** *is also a type of Scottish or Irish dance*
▶ *to* **reel** *is to walk unsteadily: what time did you reel in last night?*

reek, wreak

▶ *a* **reek** *is a strong unpleasant smell: the reek of rotting fish*
▶ *to* **reek** *is to smell unpleasantly*
▶ *to* **wreak** *is to carry out or cause: wreak havoc; wreak vengeance*

retch, wretch

▶ *to* **retch** *is to have the stomach spasms and make the sound of vomiting, but without actually vomiting*
▶ *a* **wretch** *is a miserable or worthless person: a lonely old wretch; an ungrateful wretch*

review, revue

▶ *to* **review** *is to give an opinion of or consider again*
▶ *a* **review** *is a critical assessment of something: a book review*
▶ *a* **review** *is also a reconsideration of something: a review of the current rules*
▶ *a* **revue** *is a theatre show with short sketches or plays*

right, rite, wright, write

▶ **right** *is an adjective with meanings such as 'correct', 'good', 'straight' and 'just': the right answer; the right thing to do*
▶ **right** *also means 'the opposite of left'*
▶ *a* **right** *is something a person is entitled to: the right to vote*
▶ *to* **right** *is to fix or set in order: to right a wrong*
▶ *a* **rite** *is a solemn religious ceremony: the rite of marriage*
▶ *a* **rite of passage** *is an event that marks a person's change of status in society, especially the entering of adulthood*
▶ *a* **wright** *is someone who makes something: a shipwright; a playwright*

▶ to **write** is to form letters with a pen or pencil or on a keyboard, or to compose a letter, article or book: *write your address down for me; he wants to write the great English novel*

ring, wring

▶ a **ring** is a round piece of jewellery worn on the finger or in the ear: *an engagement ring*
▶ a **ring** is a circle or an enclosed space: *a boxing ring*
▶ to **ring** is to go round or surround: *policemen ring the protesters*
▶ a **ring** is also the sound of a bell
▶ to **ring** is to strike or make the sound of a bell
▶ to **ring** is also to telephone: *I'll ring you when I know what the arrangements are*
▶ a **ring** is a telephone call
▶ to **wring** is to twist or squeeze: *wring the towel and then hang it on the line; I'd like to wring his neck!*
▶ to **wring** your hands is to clasp and unclasp them because of anxiety or unhappiness
▶ to **wring** money from someone is to force them to give it to you

role, roll

▶ a **role** is a part played by an actor: *a leading role in a Hollywood film*
▶ a **role model** is someone who is considered to be a good example of how to behave
▶ to **roll** is to move by turning over and over
▶ a **roll** is a very small loaf of bread
▶ a **roll** is also a list of names: *the school roll*

root, route

▶ the **root** of a plant is the part that is underground
▶ to **root** out something is to get rid of it completely: *the need to root out police corruption*
▶ to **root** is to search: *I started to root about in my papers*
▶ to **root for** a team is to support them and cheer them on

- ▶ a **route** is the course to be followed to get to a place: *the quickest route from Stirling to Inverness*
- ▶ to **route** something is to fix its route: *the council is keen to route the march away from the city centre*

rye, wry

- ▶ **rye** is a kind of grain: *rye bread*
- ▶ **wry** means 'slightly mocking': *a wry sense of humour*

sail, sale

- ▶ a **sail** is a canvas sheet that catches the wind on a boat
- ▶ a **sail** is also a journey on a boat
- ▶ to **sail** is to steer a boat or take a trip on a boat: *she's learning to sail*
- ▶ a **sale** is the exchange of anything for money
- ▶ a **sale** is also an occasion when goods are sold at reduced prices: *a closing-down sale*

scene, seen

- ▶ a **scene** is the place where something happens: *the crime scene*
- ▶ a **scene** is also a view
- ▶ a **scene** is one of the parts a play is divided into: *I'm on at the start of the third scene*
- ▶ **seen** is the past participle of the verb 'see': *have you seen my keys anywhere?*

scull, skull

- ▶ a **scull** is a short oar used to row a boat
- ▶ to **scull** is to make a boat move by rowing sculls
- ▶ the **skull** is the bony case around the brain: *a fractured skull*

sea, see

- ▶ the **sea** is the mass of salt water that covers most of the surface of the Earth
- ▶ a **sea** is a great stretch of water that is smaller than an ocean: *the North Sea*
- ▶ to **see** is to become aware of by using the eye: *I can see the bus coming now*
- ▶ a **see** is the district controlled by a bishop

seam, seem
- ▶ a **seam** is the line made when you join two pieces of material together
- ▶ a **seam** is also a layer of coal in the ground: *a rich new seam*
- ▶ to **seem** is to appear or appear to be: *he doesn't seem to be happy*

sear, seer
- ▶ to **sear** is to burn or scorch
- ▶ to **sear** is also to hurt badly: *he felt the pain sear his neck*
- ▶ a **seer** is someone who claims to be able to predict the future

sew, so, sow
- ▶ to **sew** is to join material together by means of a needle and thread
- ▶ **so** is an adverb meaning 'to such an extent': *the girls have grown so tall*
- ▶ to **sow** seeds is to scatter them over an area so that they grow: *we will need to sow more grass seed on the lawn*

shear, sheer
- ▶ to **shear** is to cut wool from a sheep
- ▶ to **shear** is also to cut through or off: *from that distance the arrows could shear through armour*
- ▶ **shears** are large scissors
- ▶ a **sheer** slope is very steep
- ▶ a **sheer** emotion is one that is not mixed in any way: *sheer misery*
- ▶ a **sheer** fabric is very thin
- ▶ to **sheer** is to swerve and change direction

soar, sore, saw
- ▶ to **soar** is to fly high in the air
- ▶ if prices **soar**, they increase very quickly
- ▶ something **sore** is painful: *a sore shoulder*
- ▶ a **sore** is a painful inflamed area on the skin

In some accents **saw** is a homophone of **soar** and **sore**

▶ **saw** *is the past tense of the verb 'see': he saw a light in the window*

sole, soul

▶ *the* **sole** *of the foot or a shoe is the underside*
▶ *to* **sole** *a shoe is to put a new sole on it*
▶ **sole** *means 'only': the sole survivor of the accident*
▶ *a* **sole** *is a type of edible fish: Dover sole*
▶ *the* **soul** *is the part of a person that is not the body: your immortal soul*
▶ *a* **soul** *is a person: she hasn't a soul in the world*
▶ **soul** *or* **soul music** *is a kind of music that combines blues, gospel, jazz and pop*

some, sum

▶ **some** *means 'several', 'a few', 'a little' and 'certain': some bananas; some sugar for my coffee; some people are bullies*
▶ *a* **sum** *is an amount made by adding numbers together*
▶ *a* **sum** *is also a quantity of money: quite a large sum is missing*
▶ *to* **sum up** *is to bring together all the points that have been made previously*

son, sun

▶ *a* **son** *is a male child*
▶ *the* **sun** *is the round object in the sky that gives the Earth heat and light*

soot, suit

▶ **soot** *is the black powder left by smoke*
▶ *a* **suit** *is a set of clothes to be worn together*
▶ *the* **suits** *are the four groups that playing cards are divided into*
▶ *to* **suit** *is to be convenient for: that time doesn't suit me*
▶ *to* **suit** *also means to look well on: that colour really suits you*

stair, stare
- ▶ a **stair** is a step or a series of steps leading between levels
- ▶ to **stare** is to look at with a fixed gaze: I turned to stare at him in amazement
- ▶ a **stare** is a fixed gaze

stake, steak
- ▶ a **stake** is a strong stick that is pointed at one end
- ▶ to **stake** a claim is to try to claim ownership of something
- ▶ a **stake** is also money that is put down as a bet
- ▶ to **stake** is to risk something: she is willing to stake her reputation on this research
- ▶ if something is **at stake**, it is in great danger: there are lives at stake
- ▶ a **steak** is a thick cut of beef or fish: a fillet steak; a tuna steak

stationary, stationery
- ▶ something **stationary** is not moving: a stationary car
- ▶ **stationery** is a term for things like writing paper, envelopes and pens

steal, steel
- ▶ to **steal** is to take something that does not belong to you without the permission of the owner
- ▶ to **steal** also means to move quietly and secretly: I tried to steal away when he was asleep
- ▶ **steel** is a very hard metal made from iron and carbon
- ▶ to **steel** yourself is to get up the courage to do something difficult

storey, story
- ▶ a **storey** refers to each level or floor of a building: a three-storey house
- ▶ a **story** is an account of an event, whether it is real or imagined: I must tell you the story of our holiday; a fairy story

straight, strait
- ▶ **straight** means 'not bent or curved', 'honest', 'at once' and 'directly': a straight line; a straight answer; he went straight home; it's quickest if you go straight across the grass

- ▶ a **strait** *is a narrow strip of sea between two pieces of land*
- ▶ **straits** *are difficult circumstances: desperate straits*
- ▶ a **straitjacket** *is a jacket with arms that can be tied that is worn to stop a person using their arms*

suite, sweet

- ▶ *a* **suite** *is a number of things in a set: a three-piece suite*
- ▶ *an en* **suite** *bathroom is attached to a bedroom*
- ▶ *something* **sweet** *tastes of sugar*
- ▶ **sweet** *also means 'pleasant' and 'agreeable': sweet music; a sweet child*
- ▶ *a* **sweet** *is a small piece of a sweet substance like chocolate*
- ▶ *a* **sweet** *is a course served at the end of a meal*

swat, swot

- ▶ *to* **swat** *an insect is to hit it and kill it*
- ▶ *a* **swat** *is a device for killing insects: a fly swat*
- ▶ *to* **swot** *is to study hard: he has gone to the library to swot for his exams*
- ▶ *a* **swot** *is someone who studies hard*

tail, tale

- ▶ *a* **tail** *is the part that sticks out from the end of the spine of an animal, bird or fish*
- ▶ *to* **tail** *someone is to follow them*
- ▶ *a* **tale** *is a story: a fairy tale*
- ▶ *a* **tale** *is also a lie: he had some long tale about the dog eating his homework*

taught, taut

- ▶ **taught** *is the past tense and past participle of the verb 'teach': I taught him how to drive; he has taught history for many years*
- ▶ *something* **taut** *is pulled tight: keep the wire taut*
- ▶ *if someone looks* **taut**, *they look tense*

tea, tee

- ▶ **tea** *is a plant grown for its leaves, which are dried and prepared to make a drink: tea plantations; I would love a cup of tea*

- ▶ **tea** *is a meal taken in the afternoon or early evening*
- ▶ *in golf, the* **tee** *is the level ground at the start of a hole: the first tee*
- ▶ *a* **tee** *is also a small peg that you put the golf ball on before hitting it at the start of a hole*

team, teem
- ▶ *a* **team** *is a group of people who work or play together: the accounts team; the Rangers first team*
- ▶ *to* **team up with** *is to join together with*
- ▶ *to* **teem** *is to be full: the Isles of Scilly teem with tourists in the summer*
- ▶ *to* **teem** *is also to rain heavily*

tear, tier
- ▶ *a* **tear** *is a drop of water passed from the eye*
- ▶ *if a person is* **in tears**, *they are crying*
- ▶ *a* **tier** *is a row of seats in a theatre*
- ▶ *a* **tier** *is also a layer: a four-tier wedding cake*

there, their, they're
- ▶ **there** *means 'in that place': there's my house; put that down over there*
- ▶ **there** *is also used at the start of sentences where the real subject follows the verb: there is someone at the front door: there's going to be snow tomorrow*
- ▶ **their** *means 'belonging to them': their cat is missing*
- ▶ **they're** *is short for 'they are': they're moving to Australia*

thyme, time
- ▶ **thyme** *is a herb with a sweet smell*
- ▶ *the* **time** *is the hour of the day*
- ▶ **time** *is also the period in which something happens*
- ▶ *to* **time** *something is to see how long it takes*

tide, tied
- ▶ *the* **tide** *is the rise and fall of the level of the sea: high tide*
- ▶ **tied** *is the past tense of the verb 'tie': the cowboy tied his horse to a post outside the saloon*

tire, tyre

▶ to **tire** *is to make or become weary: please remember that he has been ill, so he does tire easily*

▶ to **tire** of *something is to become bored with it*

▶ *a* **tyre** *is a thick rubber cover that goes round a wheel*

to, too, two

▶ **to** *is a preposition that shows direction: go to bed; the road to Morocco*

▶ **too** *is an adverb meaning 'more than is wanted': it's too hot for curry; too many to count*

▶ **too** *means 'also': I want to go too*

▶ **two** *is the number between one and three: two little birds; two fat ladies*

troop, troupe

▶ *a* **troop** *is a collection of people or animals: a Scout troop; a troop of howler monkeys*

▶ **troops** *are soldiers*

▶ to **troop** *is to move as a group: the door opened and we all began to troop inside*

▶ *a* **troupe** *is a group of performers such as actors or dancers: a Portuguese cabaret troupe*

Insight

These words are both from the same French word. **Troop** came into English in the sixteenth century from *troupe*, which itself came from *troupeau* meaning 'a flock'. It could be spelt **troupe** or **troop**, but the **troop** spelling became standard. In the nineteenth century **troupe** was again taken into English from French, this time with a slightly different meaning and with the original French spelling.

vain, vane, vein

▶ *a* **vain** *person is conceited, especially about their physical appearance*

▶ **vain** *means 'useless' and 'meaningless': a vain attempt; vain promises*

- *if something is done* in vain, *it does not succeed*
- *a* vane *is a piece of metal that swings with the wind and shows its direction*
- *a* vein *is a blood vessel that carries blood towards the heart*

vale, veil
- *a* vale *is a valley: the Vale of Glamorgan*
- *a* veil *is a piece of cloth worn to hide the face*
- *to* veil *is to hide: an attempt to veil the truth*

wail, whale
In some accents **wail** and **whale** are homophones.

- *to* wail *is to cry in sorrow*
- *a* wail *is a sad cry*
- *a* whale *is a very large mammal that lives in the sea: the blue whale*

waist, waste
- *the* waist *is the narrow part of the human body between the ribs and the hips*
- waste *is rubbish that is thrown away*
- waste *is also the extravagant use of something: a waste of water*
- *to* waste *is to use extravagantly, without any useful result: I don't want to waste any more time on this matter*

wait, weight
- *to* wait *is to remain in expectation of something: to wait for a bus*
- *to* wait *is to put off doing something: I think you should wait a while before you phone him back*
- *a* wait *is a delay*
- weight *is the amount that anything weighs: my ideal weight*
- *a* weight *is also a burden*
- *to* weight *something is to make it heavier*

waive, wave

▶ to **waive** is to give up: *the victim has agreed to waive her right to anonymity*
▶ a **wave** is a moving ridge on top of water
▶ a **wave** is also a hand gesture used as a greeting or to attract attention
▶ to **wave** is to make this hand gesture
▶ to **wave** is also to move to and fro: *the breeze got up and the flags began to wave*

waiver, waver

▶ a **waiver** is a document that confirms a person has given up their right to something
▶ to **waver** is to be unsteady on your feet
▶ to **waver** is also to be uncertain or undecided: *at first I was absolutely sure I was right but now I'm beginning to waver*

watt, what

In some accents **watt** and **what** are homophones

▶ a **watt** is a unit for measuring electrical power: *a 40-watt bulb*
▶ **what** is used to show something about which a question is being asked: *what are you doing here? what time is it?*

way, weigh, whey

▶ a **way** is a passage, path or direction: *the way in; this isn't the right way*
▶ a **way** is a method or manner: *the best way to boil an egg*
▶ to **weigh** is to have a certain weight or find out the weight of something
▶ to **weigh** an anchor is to raise it

In some accents **whey** is a homophone of **way** and **weigh**

▶ **whey** is the watery part of milk that is created when you make cheese

wear, where

In some accents **wear** and **where** are homophones

- ▶ to **wear** is to be dressed in: I never wear yellow
- ▶ to **wear** is also to damage by regular use
- ▶ **wear and tear** is damage caused by regular use
- ▶ **where** means 'to or in what place': where do you think you're going? do you know where my glasses are?

we, wee

- ▶ **we** is the pronoun used by the speaker or writer when mentioning themselves together with other people: we went out for dinner last night
- ▶ **wee** is small: a wee girl

weak, week

- ▶ something **weak** is not strong: weak tea; a weak bridge; a weak argument
- ▶ a **week** is seven consecutive days: a week in New York
- ▶ the **working week** is Monday to Friday: my boss has been away all week

weal, we'll, wheel

- ▶ a **weal** is a raised mark on the skin caused by being hit
- ▶ **we'll** is short for 'we will' and 'we shall': we'll see you on Saturday; we'll be there

In some accents **wheel** is a homophone of **weal** and **we'll**

- ▶ a **wheel** is a circular frame that turns on an axle
- ▶ to **wheel** is to turn in a circle or turn suddenly

weather, whether

In some accents **weather** and **whether** are homophones

- ▶ the **weather** is the state of the atmosphere, for example heat, cold, dryness, rain, and so on
- ▶ to **weather** something difficult is to come through it: they have had to weather many problems in their marriage

▶ **whether** *is a conjunction that means 'if' or 'either if':*
*I'm not sure whether he'll be there; I'm going whether you
go or not*

weir, we're
▶ *a* **weir** *is a dam across a stream*
▶ **we're** *is short for 'we are': we're going on a bear hunt*

wet, whet
In some accents **wet** and **whet** are homophones

▶ *something* **wet** *is soaked or covered with a liquid: wet clothes*
▶ **wet** *is rainy: wet weather*
▶ *to* **wet** *is to make wet*
▶ *to* **whet** *a knife is to make it sharp*
▶ *to* **whet** *a feeling is to make it stronger: to whet the appetite*

which, witch
In some accents **which** and **witch** are homophones

▶ **which** *is used to refer to a particular person or thing: which
is your favourite food? he doesn't know which one to choose*
▶ *a* **witch** *is a woman who is believed to have magical powers*

while, wile
In some accents **while** and **wile** are homophones

▶ **while** *means 'during the time that': Nero fiddled while
Rome burned*
▶ *to* **while away** *time is to pass it pleasantly without
being bored*
▶ *a* **wile** *is a sneaky trick*
▶ **wiles** *are charming personal ways: her womanly wiles*

whine, wine
In some accents **whine** and **wine** are homophones

▶ *to* **whine** *is to make a high-pitched noise*
▶ *to* **whine** *is also to complain: all he ever does is whine*

- ▶ **wine** *is an alcoholic drink made from grapes*
- ▶ **wine** *is also a dark red colour: a wine carpet*

who's, whose
- ▶ **who's** *is short for 'who is' and 'who has': who's there? who's been sleeping in my bed?*
- ▶ **whose** *means 'belonging to whom': whose phone is this? a girl whose brother is in my class*

wood, would
- ▶ *a* **wood** *is a group of trees growing together*
- ▶ **wood** *is the hard material underneath the bark of a tree, used for making things: cedar wood*
- ▶ **would** *is a form of the verb 'will' used to express a condition or for emphasis: I would tell you if I knew; I would love to be there*

yoke, yolk
- ▶ *a* **yoke** *is a frame used to join oxen or horses together for pulling a plough*
- ▶ *the* **yolk** *of an egg is the yellow part*

Is it spelt or spelled?

Some English words can be spelt in more than one way, so how do you know which spelling to use?

Alternative spellings are explained below and guidance is given on which to choose.

ageing and aging
Both these words are correct but **ageing** is preferred in British English and **aging** is preferred in American English: *ageing parents*.

blond or blonde
A man or boy with fair hair is **blond** or a **blond**. A woman or girl with fair hair is **blonde** or a **blonde**. When you are talking

about fair hair in general, without referring to a person of either gender, you usually spell it with the final e: *typically Scandinavian blonde hair*.

burned and burnt
Both spellings are correct but **burnt** is more common in British English and **burned** is more common in American English: *burnt toast; I burnt his letters*.

czar, tsar and tzar
Czar, **tsar** and **tzar** are all words for the former ruler of the Russian empire. The word used in Russian is *tsar*, which comes ultimately from Latin *Caesar*, meaning 'emperor', and is related to the German word *Kaiser*. British writers tend to opt for the **tsar** spelling while American writers prefer **czar**. This is also the case when the word is used to refer to an important public official with a particular responsibility, for example *business tsar* and *drugs tsar*. **Tzar** is the rarest of the three.

disc and disk
A **disc** is something that is flat and round, for example a compact disc or a record. The individual pieces that make up the spine are **discs**: *a slipped disc*. But in the context of computing, the flat round thing for storing data is a **disk**, and the part of a computer that is connected with reading and writing data on disks is the **disk drive**.

divorcé and divorcée
A man who is divorced is a **divorcé** and a woman who is divorced is a **divorcée**.

dreamed and dreamt
Both spellings are correct but **dreamt** is commoner in British English and **dreamed** is commoner in American English: *I always dreamt of living in New York*.

dwelled and dwelt
Both spellings are correct but **dwelt** is commoner in British English and **dwelled** is commoner in American English: *her speech dwelt on the need to fight inequality and poverty*.

encyclopaedia and encyclopedia

The original spelling is **encyclopædia**, and this is still used in the name of the famous *Encyclopædia Britannica*. As with **mediæval**, the **æ** became **ae** and the spelling **encyclopaedia** became standard. However, the simplified form **encyclopedia** is now the preferred spelling in British as well as American English: *an encyclopedia of gardening*.

enquire and inquire

It was previously considered correct to use **enquire** (and **enquiry**) for the general meaning of 'ask' and **inquire** (and **inquiry**) for the more formal sense of 'investigate' (and 'investigation'): *The Nolan Inquiry*. However, this distinction is no longer strictly observed and it is acceptable to use either spelling for both senses, although it should be noted that **inquire** and **inquiry** are now the preferred spellings in Britain, and **enquire** and **enquiry** are rarely used at all in American English.

fetus and foetus

The original spelling is **fœtus**, which then became **foetus**. However, nowadays the preferred form is **fetus**, in both medical and general writing, in Britain and in the United States.

homeopathy and homoeopathy

The original spelling is **homœopathy**, which then became **homoeopathy**. The preferred spelling in both British and American English is now the simplified version **homeopathy**.

instal and install

Install and **instal** are both correct spellings but **instal** is rare: *I want to install central heating*. In British English, an **instalment** is one of the parts that a debt or a serial is divided into: *we will have to pay for the central heating in instalments*. This is spelt **installment** in American English.

jail and gaol

Both **jail** and **gaol** are correct spellings of the word that means 'prison' or 'imprison'. They are both derived from an Old French word *jaiole*, meaning 'cage', but each word developed in a different part of France, before being incorporated into English. The **jail** spelling is the one used in American English, and both are still used in British English, although **jail** is now by far the commoner spelling: *a three-year jail sentence.*

judgement and judgment
In British English, the preferred form is **judgement,** although **judgment** is also found. Americans used **judgment,** for example in the title of the film *Terminator 2: Judgment Day.*

kneeled and knelt
Both spellings are correct but **knelt** is commoner in British English and **kneeled** is commoner in American English: *the woman knelt by the body of her dead husband.*

knowledgeable and knowledgable
Both of these are correct but **knowledgeable** is far commoner: *Boxing fans are very knowledgeable about the sport.*

leaned and leant
Both spellings are correct but **leant** is commoner in British English and **leaned** is commoner in American English: *I leant my bike against the wall.*

leaped and leapt
Both spellings are correct but **leapt** is commoner in British English and **leaped** is commoner in American English: *The child ran to the edge of the pool and leapt straight in.*

learned and learnt
Both spellings are correct but **learnt** is commoner in British English and **learned** is commoner in American English: *I learnt to bake from my grandmother.* However, the adjective meaning 'having great knowledge' is **learned:** *a learned philosopher.*

loveable and lovable
Lovable and **loveable** are both valid spellings, but **lovable** is commoner in both British and American English: *a lovable rogue.*

mediaeval and medieval
This word is derived from New Latin *medium aevum* meaning 'the middle age' and it was originally written **mediæval** which became **mediaeval**. However, in recent years the **mediaeval** spelling has fallen out of favour as the **ae** has been replaced in a number of words by **e**. **Mediaeval** is still correct but most British writers nowadays prefer **medieval**, which is also the preferred American spelling: *medieval literature*.

queueing and queuing
Both spellings are correct but **queuing** is commoner in both British and American English: *they're not exactly queuing up to see this film, are they?*

smelled and smelt
Both spellings are correct but **smelt** is commoner in British English and **smelled** is commoner in American English: *the house smelt damp and dusty.*

spelled and spelt
Both spellings are correct but **spelt** is commoner in British English and **spelled** is commoner in American English: *Conor spelt with one 'n'; he spelt out his plans for fighting climate change.*

spilled and spilt
Both spellings are correct but **spilt** is commoner in British English and **spilled** is commoner in American English: *spilt milk; I spilt red wine on his white shirt.*

spoiled and spoilt
Both spellings are correct but **spoilt** is commoner in British English and **spoiled** is commoner in American English: *that dog is spoilt rotten; the view was spoilt by electricity pylons.*

straight-laced and strait-laced
The original spelling is **strait-laced**, coming from an obsolete adjective sense of **strait**, meaning 'tight'. Confusion between **strait**

and **straight** gave rise to the variant **straight-laced,** which has been used for so long that it is considered standard. However, **strait-laced** is still the more commonly used form: *one of the world's most strait-laced societies.*

whiskey and whisky
Both these words refer to the alcoholic drink distilled from grain. **Whisky,** without the **e,** is the one from Scotland: *Scotch whisky.* **Whiskey,** with the **e,** is the one from Ireland or America. In British English, the spelling used is **whisky,** unless you are talking about the American or Irish spirit.

Which is it?

Some English words sound so similar to others, it's easy to get them mixed up. Below is a list of words that are often confused because of the closeness of their pronunciations, with an explanation of when to use which one.

accept and except
- ▶ to **accept** *is to take something that has been offered: he offered me money but I couldn't accept it.*
- ▶ to **accept** *also means to agree to: do you accept the conditions attached to the offer?*
- ▶ **except** *means 'not counting': our director ignores everyone except the senior managers*

access and excess
- ▶ **access** *is a way of entering or gaining or the right to enter or gain: everyone should have access to education*
- ▶ **excess** *is going beyond what is normal, proper or allowed: an excess of caffeine; excess baggage*

advice and advise
- ▶ **advice** *is something said in order to help a person in some way: diet advice*

- ▶ to **advise** *is to give advice: I advise you to speak to
  a lawyer*
- ▶ *the noun is* **advice** *and the verb is* **advise**

affect and effect
- ▶ to **affect** *is to act upon or have an influence upon: this drug is
  known to affect the nervous system; hundreds of people have
  been affected by the flooding*
- ▶ *if something* **affects** *you, it makes you feel emotional: his
  death affected me deeply*
- ▶ to **affect** *is also to put on or pretend: she managed to affect a
  confidence she did not feel*
- ▶ *an* **effect** *is the result of an action: these changes have had a
  severe effect on teacher morale*
- ▶ *an* **effect** *is an impression produced: a dazzling effect created
  by make-up*
- ▶ *a person's* **effects** *are their belongings*

allot and a lot
- ▶ to **allot** *is to give a share of: you will need to allot ten minutes
  to each interviewee*
- ▶ **a lot** *is a large number or amount of: a lot of people; a lot
  of mud*

allude and elude
- ▶ to **allude** *to something is to refer to it in passing: she did
  allude to her first marriage on more than one occasion*
- ▶ to **elude** *is to avoid: for years he has managed to
  elude capture*
- ▶ to **elude** *is to be too difficult to obtain, understand or
  remember: success in America continues to elude him*

allusion and illusion
- ▶ *an* **allusion** *is an indirect reference to something: an allusion
  to Greek mythology*
- ▶ *an* **illusion** *is something that is intended to trick the eye
  or the brain: white walls and mirrors can create an illusion
  of space in a room*

▶ an **illusion** *is also a false belief: we are under no illusions about the seriousness of the financial crisis*

allusive and elusive
▶ **allusive** *means 'hinting' or 'referring indirectly': a sly allusive remark*
▶ **elusive** *means 'difficult to catch': the famously elusive Loch Ness Monster*

bathos and pathos
▶ **bathos** *is a sudden change from a serious subject or style to a trivial one*
▶ **pathos** *is a quality that makes people feel pity: the pathos of two lonely people falling in love*

biannual and biennial
▶ *a* **biannual** *event happens twice a year: our biannual rugby club disco*
▶ *a* **biennial** *event happens once every two years: the Ryder Cup is a biennial competition*

born and borne
Born and **borne** are both past participles of the verb 'bear', but they are used differently

▶ *when the verb is active (that is, when the subject of the sentence is performing the action), the form to use is* **borne**: *she has borne three sons; I don't think that tree has ever borne fruit; crowded trains had borne the soldiers to the front; the north has borne the brunt of the recession*
▶ **borne** *should also be used for all passive uses, except when bear means 'to give birth': the costs are borne by the taxpayers; two factors must be borne in mind; the statue was borne in a procession to the church*
▶ **born** *is used for the passive of 'bear' when it means 'give birth', unless it is followed by the preposition 'by', in which case* **borne** *is used: I was born at home; has her baby been born yet? he refused to acknowledge the son borne by a local girl*

breath and breathe
- ▶ **breath** *is the air taken into and sent out of the lungs, and a* **breath** *is an instance of doing this*
- ▶ *a* **breath** *is also a slight breeze: a breath of air*
- ▶ *to* **breathe** *is to take air into the lungs and then send it out again*
- ▶ **breath** *is the noun and* **breathe** *is the verb*

concert and consort
- ▶ *a* **concert** *is a musical performance*
- ▶ *if two people or groups act* **in concert,** *they work together for some purpose*
- ▶ *a* **consort** *is a husband or wife or companion: the Queen's consort*
- ▶ *to* **consort with** *is to associate with: he accused me of consorting with criminals*

confidant, confidante and confident
- ▶ *a* **confidant** *or* **confidante** *is a person you entrust with a secret; a* **confidant** *is a man and a* **confidante** *is a woman*
- ▶ *a* **confident** *person is one who is very self-assured: a confident public speaker*
- ▶ *to be* **confident** *is also to be certain about the outcome of something: do you feel confident about the result of next Saturday's game?*

crevasse and crevice
- ▶ *a* **crevasse** *is a deep split in snow or ice*
- ▶ *a* **crevice** *is a narrow opening: creatures hide in crevices under the rock*

Insight

Both **crevasse** and **crevice** come from the same Old French word *crevace*, meaning 'crack'. But **crevice** came into English in the fourteenth century and **crevasse** arrived 500 years later, with a slightly different spelling, and a more specific meaning.

defuse and diffuse

▶ to **defuse** *a bomb is to make it safe by removing the fuse*
▶ to **defuse** *a situation is to make it less tense or dangerous: ways to defuse racial tension*
▶ to **diffuse** *is to spread out in all directions: a frosted shade to diffuse the light*
▶ **diffuse** *means 'widely spread': a geographically diffuse support*

device and devise

▶ *a* **device** *is a tool or instrument: an explosive device*
▶ to **leave a person to their own devices** *is to leave them alone to do what they want*
▶ to **devise** *is to put together or plan: we need to devise a fairer system for payments*
▶ **device** *is the noun and* **devise** *is the verb*

elicit and illicit

▶ to **elicit** *is to draw something out from a person: a blatant attempt to elicit sympathy; my questions elicited no useful response*
▶ *something* **illicit** *is illegal or forbidden: an illicit copy of the photograph; illicit drugs*

emigrate and immigrate

▶ to **emigrate** *is to leave your own country and go to live in another country: we have decided to emigrate*
▶ to **immigrate** *to a country is to go and live there: my parents immigrated here more than 30 years ago*
▶ *To know which one to use is a matter of position: if someone goes away from where you live, they are* **emigrating**; *if they come to where you live, they are* **immigrating**.

Insight

Emigrate is from the Latin *ex* meaning 'out' and *mīgrāre* meaning 'to move'. **Immigrate** is from the Latin *im* meaning 'in' and *mīgrāre*. Therefore, to **emigrate** is to move out and to **immigrate** is to move in.

eminent and imminent
- ▶ *an* **eminent** *person is famous and respected: an eminent surgeon*
- ▶ *something* **imminent** *is about to happen: the imminent election*

ensure and insure
- ▶ *to* **ensure** *is to make sure: you must ensure that the doors and windows are locked when you go on holiday*
- ▶ *to* **insure** *is to arrange for a sum of money to be paid if something is lost, stolen or damaged: you ought to insure your jewellery separately if it is valuable; many companies won't insure your house if you live on a flood plain*

excerpt and exert
- ▶ *an* **excerpt** *is a part taken from a larger work: an excerpt from 'The Magic Flute'*
- ▶ *to* **exert** *is to use or apply: Oberon tries to exert his authority*
- ▶ *to* **exert oneself** *is to make a big physical or mental effort*

exercise and exorcize
- ▶ **exercise** *is physical training such as running done in order to become fitter or healthier*
- ▶ *an* **exercise** *is a task done to get practice at something: a military exercise*
- ▶ *to* **exercise** *is to take physical exercise*
- ▶ *to* **exercise** *is also to use or apply: to exercise authority*
- ▶ *to* **exorcize** *is to drive out an evil spirit*

ferment and foment
- ▶ *when a substance* **ferments**, *it undergoes a chemical reaction so that alcohol is produced*
- ▶ *if you* **ferment** *trouble, you cause it*
- ▶ *if trouble* **ferments**, *it happens*
- ▶ *if you* **foment** *trouble, you stir it up: to foment rebellion*

forego and forgo
- ▶ *to* **forgo** *is to do without something: all staff have been asked to forgo bonuses and pay rises this year*
- ▶ *to* **forego** *is to come before in time*

- *the verb* **forego** *is itself not that common but two of its forms are:* **foregoing**, *which means 'preceding'; and* **foregone**, *as in the phrase* **foregone** conclusion, *which is a result that can be predicted in advance*
- **forgo** *can also be spelt as* **forego**, *but the* **forgo** *spelling is more common*

foreword and forward
- *a* **foreword** *is an introduction at the start of a book*
- **forward** *means 'towards the front': time to go forward; a forward rush*

inapt and inept
- *something* **inapt** *is unsuitable or inappropriate: the name Grace is singularly inapt in her case*
- **inept** *means 'clumsy or badly done': an inept display of goalkeeping; the inept way the management dealt with the complaints*

ingenious and ingenuous
- *an* **ingenious** *person is clever at inventing things*
- *something* **ingenious** *has been cleverly planned or made: an ingenious thriller*
- *an* **ingenuous** *person is honest and trusting*

interment and internment
- **interment** *is the burial of a dead body*
- **internment** *is the imprisonment of people, especially during a war*

lair and layer
- *a* **lair** *is the den of a wild animal*
- *a* **layer** *is a quantity of some material on top of something or between two other things: a thick layer of snow; a layer of jam between two sponge cakes*

lath and lathe
- *a* **lath** *is a narrow strip of wood*
- *a* **lathe** *is a machine for shaping things from wood or metal*

liqueur and liquor

▶ a **liqueur** *is a type of strong sweet alcoholic drink*
▶ **liquor** *is a name for any alcoholic drink or for alcoholic drinks collectively: I never touch liquor*

loath, loathe and loth

▶ **loath** *and* **loth** *both mean 'unwilling': he is loath to talk about his first marriage; I'm loth to buy a new car*
▶ *to* **loathe** *is to hate: I loathe weddings*

loose and lose

▶ *something that is* **loose** *is not tight or firmly attached: a loose jacket; the bull is loose*
▶ *to* **loose** *is to make loose or untie: loose the sail*
▶ *to* **lose** *is to cease to have: I'm about to lose my job; when did you lose your mobile phone?*

moral and morale

▶ *the* **moral** *of a story is the lesson it teaches*
▶ **morals** *are the standards of behaviour that a person observes*
▶ **moral** *means 'relating to the understanding of what is right and wrong': a moral decision*
▶ **morale** *is the level of confidence felt by a person or group: morale among troops is high despite the dangerous conditions*

Insight

The word **moral** has been established in English since the fourteenth century. It comes from the Latin word *moralis* which means 'of or relating to customs'. **Morale** came into English from French in the eighteenth century, and it is a form of the adjective **moral**, which had taken on this specific meaning.

motif and motive

▶ a **motif** *is a recurring shape in a design: a thistle motif*
▶ *the* **motif** *of a piece of music or writing is its main feature or idea: the prison motif in 'Little Dorrit'*
▶ a **motive** *is a reason for a person's actions: the motive for the crime appears to be robbery*

parameter and perimeter

- ▶ *the parameters of something are the factors that limit what can be done: the parameters of what is acceptable on television*
- ▶ *the perimeter is the outside line or edge of a figure or an area: soldiers with dogs patrolled the camp perimeter*

personal and personnel

- ▶ *something personal belongs to a person for their own private use: a personal computer; personal papers*
- ▶ *a personal remark is deliberately insulting*
- ▶ *the personnel of an organization are the people who work for it*
- ▶ *the personnel department of an organization is responsible for the welfare of the staff*

precede and proceed

- ▶ *to precede is to be or go before in time, place or importance: the political unrest that preceded the war*
- ▶ *to proceed is to begin or continue to do something: the government agreed to proceed with a referendum on the treaty; the teacher paused at the interruption and then proceeded*

premier and première

- ▶ *the premier is the leader of a country*
- ▶ *a premier person or thing is a very important one: a premier advertising agency; the premier prize in women's tennis*
- ▶ *the première of a film or a play is its first performance*

preposition and proposition

- ▶ *a preposition is a type of word that is used to show the relation between words, for example under, of, on and past*
- ▶ *a proposition is a suggestion or a statement: is working at home really a practical proposition for you?*

prescribe and proscribe

- ▶ *to prescribe a medicine is to order a patient to take it*
- ▶ *to prescribe is also to make a rule: it is not possible to prescribe a single policy to suit all circumstances*

▶ to **proscribe** *is to prohibit or ban: a number of his books were proscribed by the Soviet authorities*

prophecy and prophesy
▶ *a* **prophecy** *is a foretelling of what will happen in the future: a prophecy of doom*
▶ *to* **prophesy** *is to predict the future*
▶ **prophecy** *is the noun and* **prophesy** *is the verb*

quiet and quite
▶ *someone or something* **quiet** *makes little or no noise*
▶ *a* **quiet** *place has few people or little traffic*
▶ **quiet** *is a lack of noise: I love the quiet of the countryside*
▶ *to* **quiet** *is to make or become quiet*
▶ **quite** *is an adverb that means 'moderately' or 'totally': he's quite good, I suppose; I quite agree with Simon on this*

reverend and reverent
▶ **reverend**, *which means 'worthy of respect', is a title given to members of the clergy: Reverend Patrick Bronte*
▶ **reverent** *means 'showing respect': a reverent silence*

sceptic and septic
▶ *a* **sceptic** *is a person who does not tend to believe what they are told*
▶ *a* **septic** *wound is infected with bacteria*

silicon and silicone
▶ **silicon** *is an element that is used to make silicon chips for computers*
▶ **silicone** *is an artificial substance used in breast implants*

surplice and surplus
▶ *a* **surplice** *is a loose white robe worn by some clergymen*
▶ *a* **surplus** *is an amount left over that is not needed: grout the tiles and wipe off any surplus; surplus fat*

swingeing and swinging

▶ swingeing *means 'very great or severe' and comes from an old-fashioned verb* swinge *which means 'to beat or punish': a swingeing attack on the BBC; swingeing cuts in public spending*

▶ swinging *is the present participle of the verb 'swing': swinging the briefcase back and forth*

teeth and teethe

▶ teeth *is the plural of 'tooth': everyone on television nowadays has incredibly white teeth*

▶ *when a baby starts to* teethe, *its first teeth start to come through its gums*

▶ teeth *is the plural noun and* teethe *is the verb*

venal and venial

▶ *a* venal *person is corrupt and can be bribed: venal politicians*

▶ *a* venial *sin is not very serious and can be forgiven*

veracious and voracious

▶ *a* veracious *person is truthful*

▶ *a* voracious *person has an enormous appetite for something, very often food: voracious hunger; a voracious reader*

Exercise

There are words missing from the following passage that can all be found and explained in Chapter 8. Can you work out which words they are and be sure you are inserting the correct spelling?

The school athletics ___ recently took part in a national competition. It was ___ an adventure. The school ___ asked for parents to help out and I volunteered. I was the only one with a clean driving ___ so I ended up driving the minibus, which had been leant to us by the local ___. We also had to ___ the money

(Contd)

needed to pay for the trip. We did this by having a 'festive ___'
and the Women's ___ held a ___ for us in the ___ of the church.
A local businessman gave us a ___ for £200. All the ___ went into
our competition trip fund.

Meanwhile the children each had to ___ for their own event.
The competition itself was a ___ success. Although they were up
against some schools who were much more experienced than
they were, our pupils were not at all ___ by it. The organizers even
___ us on their attitude and enthusiasm. The ___ of the squad was
Helen, who won the 100 ___ and also ran the final leg of the relay
race, where she recovered from a poor ___ change to finish in
second ___.

Our team came home with no fewer than seven ___.

10-question diagnostic test

1 What is a homophone?
2 Can you name two homophones with different spellings?
3 Can you name two homophones with different meanings?
4 Can you name two homophones with different spellings and
   different meanings?
5 Which is correct: Scotch **whisky** or Scotch **whiskey**?
6 According to the book and film, do Gentlemen Prefer **Blonds**
   or **Blondes**?
7 Which is the noun: **advice** or **advise**?
8 Which is the verb: **practice** or **practise**?
9 What do you not want to do with your house keys: **lose** them or
   loose them?
10 When you have been running fast, you do have to catch your
   breath or your **breathe**?

10 THINGS TO REMEMBER

1 *A homophone is a word that sounds like another word.*

2 *The word homophone comes from Greek and literally means 'same sound'.*

3 *Homophones can have the same spelling but have different meanings.*

4 *Homophones can have the same meaning but have different spellings.*

5 *Homophones can have different meanings as well as different spellings.*

6 *In many accents of British English,* **wh** *at the beginning of a word sounds the same as* **w.**

7 *Many words can be spelt in more than one way but most have one spelling that is preferred over the other.*

8 *For some words, British English opts for one spelling, while American English opts for another.*

9 *In word pairs like* **advice** *and* **advise,** **licence** *and* **license,** *and* **prophecy** *and* **prophesy,** *the noun is the one with the letter* **c** *and the verb is the one with the letter* **s.**

10 *In word pairs like* **breath** *and* **breathe,** **loath** *and* **loathe,** *and* **teeth** *and* **teethe,** *the verb is the one with the final* **e.**

9

Memory tricks

In this chapter you will learn:
- *how mnemonics are very useful when it comes to spelling tricky words*
- *about initial, partial and whole-word mnemonics*
- *how to create your own mnemonics.*

Many people use rhymes or lines to remember how to spell certain words. A memory prompt like this is called a **mnemonic**. This word, which is pronounced /ni-**nom**-ik/, comes from the Greek *mnēmonikos*, which means 'mindful', coming from the verb *mnasthai*, meaning 'to remember'.

Most of us already use mnemonics to remember a variety of things. For example, the verse that begins with the line 'Thirty days has September' is a mnemonic for remembering how many days are in each month. The colours of the rainbow in their correct order can be recalled by using the line 'Richard of York gave battle in vain' (red, orange, yellow, green, blue, indigo and violet). In musical notation, the notes on the treble clef are remembered by 'Every good boy deserves favour' (E, G, B, D and F). In history, the five Privy Counsellors who advised King Charles II became known as the Cabal – Clifford, Arlington, Buckingham, Ashley-Cooper and Lauderdale. And the one rule of English spelling that almost everyone knows is itself a mnemonic: 'i before e except after c'.

Mnemonics are very useful when it comes to spelling. There are a number of quite well-known ones but the beauty of mnemonics is that you can make up your own and the only thing that matters is that they work for you. If there are certain words that always cause you problems, try to make up a mnemonic for each of them. You can create different kinds.

Initial mnemonics

Can you make a phrase or sentence in which each word begins with one letter in the problem word? This is obviously harder for longer words. It helps if you can make the sentence or phrase relate to the word itself, as with most of these below, for example **beige** and **easel**. This is because a totally random string of words is no easier to remember than a string of letters! Here are some examples, using words from the list in Chapter 6:

anoint	**a**nd **n**ow **o**il **i**s **n**eatly **t**ransferred
autumn	**a**n **u**mbrella **t**ells **u**s **m**eteorological **n**ews
beautiful	**b**ig **e**lephants **a**re **u**seful **t**o **I**ndians **f**or **u**nloading **l**ogs

beauty	**b**ig **e**ars **a**re **u**nflattering **t**o **y**ouths
because	**b**ig **e**lephants **c**annot **u**se **s**mall **e**ntrances
beige	**b**rown **e**xists **i**n **g**arments **e**verywhere
buoy	**b**oater **u**ntied **o**ne **y**esterday
cipher	**c**all **i**f **p**eople **h**ave **e**nigma **r**esolution
condemn	**c**riminals **o**f **N**ottingham **d**o **e**very **m**isdemeanour **n**ightly
dahlia	**d**affodils **a**re **h**ardly **l**iving **i**n **a**utumn
easel	**e**ach **a**rtist **s**tands **e**njoying **l**andscape
emperor	**e**very **MP** **e**xpects **r**afts **o**f **r**iches
eulogy	**e**nds **u**p **l**ying **o**ver **g**hastly **y**ob
frieze	**f**ancy **r**ooms **i**nspire **e**xtraordinary **z**igzag **e**mbellishment
gauge	**g**o **a**nd **u**se **g**reat **e**nergy
hamster	**h**ardly **a**nyone **m**entions **s**eeing **T**om **e**ating **r**at
harass	**h**ave **a** **r**eally **a**nnoying **s**mall **s**ister
hymn	**h**onour **y**our **m**aker **n**ow!
Inoculate	**i**llness **n**ow **o**nly **c**omes **u**pon **l**eprechauns **a**fter **t**errible **e**nchantment
karaoke	**K**err **a**nd **R**obert **a**re **o**utrageously **k**een **e**ntertainers
liaison	**l**isten **i**n **a**nd **i**nterrogate **s**uspicious **o**range **n**eurotic
muscle	**M**anchester **U**nited **s**triker **c**laims **l**arge **e**arnings
novel	**N**abokov's **o**dd **v**olume **e**nraged **l**adies
piquant	**p**aprika **i**s **q**uietly **u**ndermining **a** **n**utty **t**aste
prefer	**p**eople **r**arely **e**njoy **f**inding **e**lephants **r**egurgitating
recipe	**R**amsay **e**njoys **c**ursing **i**n **p**rofane **E**nglish
seize	**s**oldiers **e**ventually **i**nvade **Z**ambian **e**mpire
series	**s**ix **e**pisodes **r**an **i**n **e**vening **s**lot
sign	**s**cribbling **i**ndicates **g**iven **n**ame
symbol	**s**cribbling **y**ields **M**r **B**rown's **o**wn **l**uxury
tactic	**t**ry **a**nd **c**onquer **t**eam **i**n **c**harge
tyranny	**t**errifying **Y**ankees **r**an **N**ew **Y**ork
wilful	**w**hat **I** **l**ike **f**orms **u**nending **l**oathing

Insight

When writing these mnemonics I was inspired by a variety of sources, including MPs' expenses, Freddie Starr, the sequel to *The Da Vinci Code*, a sweary TV chef and Terry Wogan.

Partial mnemonics

These mnemonics reinforce the spelling of only part of the word.
They focus on the part of the word that is hardest to spell, whether
it is because of a silent letter (for example **abscess**), or because of
a mixture of double and single letters (for example **paraffin**), or
because there may be some difference between the pronunciation
and the spelling (for example **despair**). They may remind the writer
of the word's similarity to another word (for example **niece** and
piece) or point out a smaller word within the word in question
(for example **hurt** in **yoghurt**).

abscess	there is a **sca**b on your ab**sc**ess

> **Insight**
>
> I know this abscess mnemonic is rather revolting but I think
> it's quite a useful one, and it also illustrates the point that the
> ruder and cruder something is, the easier it is to remember.

apparent	something a**ppar**ent is **p**erfectly **p**lain
bellwether	the bell**wether** leads a **wet her**d of sheep
broccoli	**Rocco** loves b**rocco**li
business	we find bu**si**ness **sin**ful
committee	the co**mmittee** has two **M**exicans, two **T**urks and two **E**gyptians
contour	the **tour**ists enjoyed a **tour** of the con**tour**s of the mountain
definite	it is **finite** as well as de**finite**
despair	if you are in **desp**air you are **desp**erate
environment	we are worried about the amount of **iron** in the env**iron**ment
furore	there was a **furore** about the **fur** coat the model w**ore**
innocuous	an in**no**cuous comment is **no**t **n**asty
interrupt	it is **r**eally **r**ude to inter**r**upt
jeopardy	the l**eopard** is in j**eopard**y
kerosene	keep **Rose** from the ke**rose**ne
naive	it's n**aive** to w**aive** your claim to the money

niece	the niece takes a piece of pie
origin	the origin of gin
paraffin	don't feed the giraffe paraffin
pavilion	there was a lion in the pavilion
peccadillo	a peccadillo is a common crime or a little lapse
portrait	a portrait of a traitor
quarter	a quart is a quarter of a gallon
relief	he had to lie flat out in relief
reminiscent	it is reminiscent of the scent of a mini
ricochet	a ricochet killed Rico and Chet Atkins
satellite	a satellite has one turbine and two laser lights
scene	Scott made a scary scene
schedule	do you have a schedule for school?
scissors	scissors and scalpels are scarily sharp
shoulder	you should push with your shoulder
sovereign	long may the foreign sovereign reign
stationery	envelopes are stationery
strategy	I don't rate your strategy
success	they enjoyed success in the Calcutta Cup
tournament	that player made his name in last year's tournament
yoghurt	yoghurt won't hurt you

Whole-word mnemonics

With these, the tricky word is spelt out entirely across at least two consecutive words, rather in the style of a crossword clue.

allege	they allege he is a criminal legend
bias	there is a bias against the Serbia squad
calendar	can Monica lend a reminder for the calendar?
defendant	the lawyer is not keen to defend Anthony as a defendant
dependent	being dependent is to depend entirely on other people
diamond	you'll get the diamond from India Monday morning
digit	does your digit dig it?
disaster	disaster struck Candi's asteroid
dynasty	the Scottish royal dynasty found the first King Eddy nasty

effete	a bri**ef fete** makes one effete
enthral	the sev**enth ral**ly did not enthral me
espresso	caf**es press o**rganic coffee for espresso
flour	**Flo ur**ges the dough to rise
kernel	that's the kernel of the con**ker, Nel**ly
lyric	the lyric is actual**ly Ric**k Astley's
obsess	please don't obsess over whether your j**ob's ess**ential
ochre	the l**och re**ally looks ochre in this light
often	I often sit above the l**oft en**trance
pastel	a pastel is the colour of **past el**egance
privilege	I find the privilege of living in Ca**pri vile, Ge**rry
risotto	the risotto on the floor **is Otto**'s
shepherd	the shepherd and his dog **Shep herd** the sheep together
tongue	the wan**ton gue**st choked on his tongue
tourist	the tourist says the **tour is t**remendous
tragedy	Hamle**t raged y**et it was still a tragedy
traitor	being a traitor is a bad **trait, Or**son
vitamin	I don't have the vitamin pill, I passed Gav **it a min**ute ago

Insight

You may find it helpful to you use your word-within-a-word strategy from Chapter 3 for composing these kinds of mnemonics.

Tips for creating your own mnemonics

▶ *Give them some meaning – you're unlikely to remember a list of unrelated words.*

▶ *If you can, connect the word's meaning to the mnemonic in some way.*

▶ *If you're writing partial mnemonics, concentrate on the tricky bits.*

▶ *Include the names of people you know (for example Gav, Robert, Tom).*

▶ *Use subjects that interest you (for example Hamlet, Manchester United, Rick Astley).*

▶ *The more personal the mnemonic is to you, the more likely you are to remember and use it.*

Exercise

The following sentences each have a word from Chapter 6 hidden as a mnemonic within them. Can you find the word in each?

1 *Are your friends actually real, Lynne?*
2 *He's not as tall as the chap I met recently.*
3 *It's time to reignite the debate about the monarchy.*
4 *A country cottage on the River Ural.*
5 *If she doesn't know the answer, Ava guesses.*
6 *Has evil lain within his heart all this time?*
7 *You should give this culinary custom a chance.*
8 *She saves tigers from poachers, the few that remain.*
9 *Put the can in the locker between eight and ten.*
10 *I don't think Ivor Novello wrote books.*

Exercise

See if you can write your own mnemonics for some of the words in Chapter 6.

10-question diagnostic test

1 *What is a mnemonic?*
2 *What language does the word come from?*
3 *What does it mean?*
4 *What is the mnemonic for the colours of the rainbow?*
5 *What is the mnemonic for the notes of the treble clef?*
6 *What is the mnemonic for Charles II's Privy Counsellors?*
7 *What is the best-known spelling mnemonic?*
8 *What kind of mnemonic is this: there is a bias against the*
   Ser**bia s**quad?
9 *What kind of mnemonic is this:* **Rocco** loves **brocco**li?
10 *What kind of mnemonic is this:* **b**oater **u**ntied **o**ne **y**esterday?

10 THINGS TO REMEMBER

1 *A mnemonic is a way of remembering something.*

2 *Mnemonics can be used for all kinds of things.*

3 *There are initial spelling mnemonics.*

4 *There are partial spelling mnemonics.*

5 *There are whole-word spelling mnemonics.*

6 *If you are creating a spelling mnemonic, try to connect the phrase or sentence to the meaning of the word.*

7 *Make the mnemonic more personal to you by using the names of people you know.*

8 *A mnemonic must have some logic to it in order to be memorable – a list of random words is no easier to remember than a list of letters.*

9 *If you are writing a partial mnemonic, concentrate on the word's tricky bits.*

10 *The ruder or more ridiculous the mnemonic, the easier it is to remember!*

10

Dictionaries and spellcheckers

In this chapter you will learn:
- *about the importance of using a dictionary in your writing*
- *how to choose the right dictionary for you*
- *about the British versus American spelling debate*
- *about the pros and cons of the computer spellchecker.*

A dictionary is a reference book that contains an alphabetical list of words with their meanings. The word **dictionary** came into English in the sixteenth century from the Medieval Latin *dictiōnārium* which means 'a collection of words'. The Latin for 'word' is *dictio*.

> **Insight**
> The first alphabetical dictionary of English was written in 1604 by Robert Cawdrey. However, Samuel Johnson's *A Dictionary of the English Language,* published in 1755, is considered to have been the first thorough and reliable dictionary of the English language.

Everyone who ever has to write something for study, work, pleasure or leisure should keep a dictionary near to hand. It is as indispensable for writing as a pen and paper, or a computer and printer. Not only does a dictionary tell you what words mean, it also offers invaluable information about how words should be used, which words to avoid and, often, where words come from. Sometimes they provide extra help in the form of synonyms (words that mean the same as the word you are looking at) and antonyms (words that mean the opposite of the word you are looking at), and even website addresses that show you where to look online if you want to find out more about a particular subject. Some dictionaries even have encyclopedia-type entries about people and places, telling you key facts about them that you may need to know, for example *What is the capital of Lithuania?* or *When did Mozart die?*

Modern dictionaries contain an astonishing variety of information, all included by the publisher in order to tempt you to buy their books.

But research undertaken by dictionary publishers has shown that the prime reason for consulting a dictionary is to check the spelling of a word. So, in spite of all the undoubtedly fascinating information to be found in modern dictionaries, people still pick them up and buy them because they want to know how to spell something.

And for that reason, if no other, everyone should use a dictionary.

Large versus small: does size matter?

Go to your nearest bookshop and you will see an impressive range of dictionaries available, from the smallest paperback that fits in a pocket to the largest hardback that is so heavy that it takes two hands to lift it off the shelf. How on earth do you decide which one to buy?

The bigger the dictionary, the more entries (headwords) it has. A large dictionary will contain many more technical, old-fashioned and unusual words than a small one. If your writing tends to contain a lot of scientific or highly specialized vocabulary, then a bigger dictionary will probably be more useful to you.

For most of us, however, the words we tend to struggle with are not necessarily highly technical. They are part of our everyday vocabulary, and the problems are caused by uncertainty over whether a letter is doubled or not, or whether the word takes an e before adding s to make a plural. Most people, myself included, would have to check a dictionary before attempting to write the full name for DNA – deoxyribonucleic acid – because we know that it is a difficult word. But I suspect that few of us often have to write words like that in the course of our daily business, whether in our work or our personal lives. We are more likely to be checking how to spell **embarrass, efficient, interrupt** or **secretary**.

For that reason, a smaller dictionary will almost always be big enough to include the words you need to check regularly. Before choosing a dictionary, you should look inside and see how big the size of the type is. A very small dictionary is likely to have quite small letters – an unfortunate but inevitable result of trying to get as many headwords as possible into a physically small book. If you find it difficult to read small type, you may want to go for something just a bit bigger.

Many dictionaries nowadays use a second colour to make them easier to read, and a lot of people find that helpful.

Dictionaries also vary in how much information they show about the other forms of the headword. By this I mean the different parts of a verb (for example, **dances, dancing, danced** and **totals, totalling, totalled**), the comparative and superlative forms of an adjective (for example, **bigger, biggest** and **spicier, spiciest**), and the plurals of nouns (for example, **potatoes** and **diaries**). You should check to see how many of these forms are shown and decide for yourself if the dictionary you are looking it is offering you as much information as you would like.

Physical versus virtual: on the page or online?

Nowadays every word processing package comes complete with a dictionary. The internet also has a wide selection of free dictionaries that you can use, as well as some that you must pay for.

If you are a scholar or a language enthusiast you can pay to access the *Oxford English Dictionary* online, which is a remarkable resource. There is no doubt that it is cheaper, quicker and easier to look up a word in the online OED than in its 20-volume paper equivalent. If you have an interest in the English language and how it has developed, then you will find the OED endlessly fascinating.

But for most people, the free online dictionaries available will be large enough to serve their needs. But, as with so many things that are free on the internet, some caution is needed.

The most important thing to check is whether the dictionary is British or American. As you will see in more detail in the next section, the differences between British and American spelling are great enough for it to matter where a dictionary originated. If you are not sure whether it is British or American, do the following test. Enter the word 'grey' in the search box. If it comes back with something like 'the British word for gray' or 'the UK word for gray' or 'an alternative spelling of gray', then the dictionary is American, not British.

It is also a good idea to make sure that any free website is using a text from a reputable dictionary publisher, such as Collins, Oxford or Chambers. Personally, I would avoid dictionaries which are open to any contributors. They may be interesting and entertaining, but I believe they lack the editorial expertise that dictionary editing requires.

So which is better? An online dictionary or its physical equivalent? That depends on the circumstances. If you are using a reliable and reputable online dictionary, then that is as good as a printed book. It's quick and easy to search. But many people prefer the security of the physical object, and take pleasure in flicking through its pages, stopping here and there when something interesting catches their eye.

Whichever camp you fall into, it's important to remember one thing. The dictionary is one of the greatest allies you have in the battle for good spelling.

British spelling versus American spelling: the big fight

It may be open to debate whether Britain and America are, as they have been described, 'two nations separated by a common language', but there is no doubting that there are significant differences between the spelling of British English and that of American English. For this reason it is essential that writers of British English ensure that they are using a British English dictionary for checking their spelling, whether the dictionary is a printed book or an online electronic version.

When you use a spellchecker in your word-processing package, make sure you select the British English option.

The differences in vocabulary between American and British English, such as **sidewalk** for **pavement, pants** for **trousers** and **diaper** for **nappy**, do not, for the most part, cause problems for speakers of either version. These alternatives are well established and recognized, and the use of the 'other' word by a native speaker is often done for deliberate effect or for humour.

Insight

One episode of the US sitcom *Friends* has two of the female characters mocking an irritating former acquaintance who has been living in London for using the term **mobile** instead of **cell**. Her adoption of the British word is seen as an affectation, as is her strained English accent.

Differences in pronunciation are also well established and generally accepted. An American will say **vase, tomato** and **oregano** as 'vayz', 'to-**may**-to' and 'o-**reg**-uh-no', and a British person will understand and make the mental translation to 'vahz', 'to-**mah**-to' and 'o-ri-**gah**-no'.

Insight

The different pronunciations of **tomato** and **potato** were celebrated in the song 'Let's Call the Whole Thing Off' written by George and Ira Gershwin.

But the area of spelling is altogether trickier and can often lead to confusion and mistakes.

There are a number of spelling patterns that are treated differently in British and American English.

OUR AND OR

Words with more than one syllable that end with an unstressed **our** in British English end with **or** in American English, for example:

UK	US
ardour	ardor
armour	armor
behaviour	behavior
candour	candor
clamour	clamor
colour	color
enamour	enamor
endeavour	endeavor
favour	favor
fervour	fervor
flavour	flavor
harbour	harbor
honour	honor
humour	humor
labour	labor
neighbour	neighbor
odour	odor
parlour	parlor
rancour	rancor
rigour	rigor
rumour	rumor
saviour	savior
savour	savor

(Contd)

UK	US
succour	succor
tumour	tumor
valour	valor
vapour	vapor
vigour	vigor

Exceptions: The *Space Shuttle Endeavour*, although American, has the British spelling because it is named after Captain James Cook's ship *HMS Endeavour*.

The spelling **glamour** is widely used in the United States, although **glamor** is also seen. This is because **glamour** is derived from Scots, and not from French or Latin, and so did not undergo the change from **our** to **or** that was laid out in Noah Webster's *American Dictionary of the English Language*, which was published in 1828, and which had the effect of fixing that, and other spellings, in American English.

Derived words that are made from these words by the addition of suffixes follow the spelling of the original word (except for those already explained in Chapter 4, for example **humour**).

It is highly probable that you see at least one of these American spellings every day, especially if your computer uses a Microsoft operating system. The toolbar on my Windows Internet Explorer has a button that allows me to return to my 'Favorites'. And at the moment my printer keeps sending messages telling me that my 'Color' is low and I need to order another cartridge. As with many internet resources, the default English spelling is American.

RE *AND* ER

British English words with more than one syllable that end with **re** preceded by letter **b**, **h**, **t** or **v**, where this last syllable is unstressed, are spelt with **er** in American English, for example:

UK	US
calibre	caliber
fibre	fiber
sabre	saber
sombre	somber
ochre	ocher
sepulchre	sepulcher
accoutre	accouter
centre	center
dioptre	diopter
goitre	goiter
lacklustre	lackluster
lustre	luster
litre	liter
metre	meter
mitre	miter
nitre	niter
philtre	philter
reconnoitre	reconnoiter
saltpetre	saltpeter
sceptre	scepter
spectre	specter
theatre	theater
louvre	louver
manoeuvre	maneuver

Exceptions: As a British English speaker, when you are writing about the *World Trade Center*, you should spell it with the American Spelling, as this was its formal name (just as Americans spell *Endeavour* in the British style).

CE *AND* SE

There is quite a lot of confusion about the spelling of some words that end with se and ce. There are two reasons for this: there is a distinction between how some related verbs and nouns are spelt; and there is a difference between how words are spelt in British and American English.

For those reasons, I have explained the tricky ones in full below.

advice or advise
In both British and American English the spellings are as follows:
advice is the noun (*I need your advice*) and **advise** is the verb
(*please can you advise me what to do*).

defence or defense
This word is a noun. It is spelt **defence** in British English
(*The Ministry of Defence*) and **defense** in American English
(*United States Department of Defense*).

device or devise
In both British and American English the spellings are as follows:
device is the noun (*a device for opening tins*) and **devise** is the verb
(*to devise a scheme to make money*).

licence or license
In British English, the noun is **licence** (*a driving licence*) and the
verb is **license** (*would you license James Bond to kill?*) In American
English, both the noun and the verb are spelt **license**: *a US driver's
license; you need to license a gun.*

Insight
The British English verb and noun have different spellings and
the American noun and verb have the same spelling as the
British verb. All this contributes to the confusion around how
to spell **licence** and **license** in British English and helps explain
why the noun **licence** is so often incorrectly written as **license**.

offence or offense
This word is a noun. It is spelt **offence** in British English (*a criminal
offence in England and Wales*) and **offense** in American English
(*an offense against the office of the President*).

practice or practise
In British English, the noun is **practice** (*I need a bit more practice
before I can play in public*) and the verb is **practise** (*I need to*

practise playing the guitar every day). In American English, both the noun and the verb are spelt **practice**: *he was late for baseball practice; if you don't practice pitching, you won't make the team.*

IZE *AND* ISE

The issue of whether to use **ize** or **ise** at the end of a verb has already been dealt with in Chapter 4 of this book. However, there are some words where American English and British English differ, for example:

UK	US
advertise	advertize
prise	prize

In American English, the verb **prize** means 'to value highly' and 'to force open'. In British English, **prize** is used for the first sense, and **prise** for the second.

YZE *AND* YSE

There are a few verbs ending with the letters **yze** in American English that must be spelt with **yse** in British English, for example:

UK	US
analyse	analyze
autolyse	autolyze
catalyse	catalyze
dialyse	dialyze
electrolyse	electrolyze
hydrolyse	hydrolyze
overanalyse	overanalyze
paralyse	paralyze
psychoanalyse	psychoanalyze
reanalyse	reanalyze

OGUE *AND* OG

There is a group of British words ending with the letters **ogue** that are spelt with **og** in American English, for example:

UK	US
analogue	analog
catalogue	catalog
demagogue	demagog
dialogue	dialog
monologue	monolog
pedagogue	pedagog

AE *AND* E

Some words that contain the letters **ae** in British English (which was originally written as **æ**) are spelt with just the letter **e** in American English, for example:

UK	US
anaemia	anemia
anaemic	anemic
anaesthesia	anesthesia
anaesthetic	anesthetic
caesium	cesium
gynaecology	gynecology
haemoglobin	hemoglobin
haemophilia	hemophilia
haemorrhage	hemorrhage
leukaemia	leukemia
orthopaedic	orthopedic
paediatric	pediatric
paedophile	pedophile

Exceptions: In current British English usage, **encyclopedia** (rather than **encyclopaedia**) and **medieval** (rather than **mediaeval**) are the preferred spellings.

OE AND E

Some words that contain the letters **oe** in British English (which was originally written as **œ**) are spelt with just the letter **e** in American English, for example:

UK	US
amoeba	ameba
diarrhoea	diarrhea
manoeuvre	maneuver
oesophagus	esophagus
oestrogen	estrogen

Exceptions: In current British English usage, **fetus** (rather than **foetus**) and **homeopathy** (rather than **homoeopathy**) are the preferred spellings.

DOUBLING FINAL LETTERS – OR NOT

A big difference between British and American spelling is the way in which final consonants behave when a suffix is added to a word. Chapter 4 explains in some detail the circumstances in which a final consonant does or does not double before adding a suffix in British English. For many of these cases the American spelling is different from the British, for example:

UK	US	UK	US
bedevilling	bedeviling	bedevilled	bedeviled
cancelling	canceling	cancelled	canceled
carolling	caroling	carolled	caroled
dialling	dialing	dialled	dialed
duelling	dueling	duelled	dueled
fuelling	fueling	fuelled	fueled
gambolling	gamboling	gambolled	gamboled
labelling	labeling	labelled	labeled
pencilling	penciling	pencilled	penciled

(Contd)

UK	US	UK	US
quarrelling	quarreling	quarrelled	quarreled
rivalling	rivaling	rivalled	rivaled
totalling	totaling	totalled	totaled
worshipping	worshiping	worshipped	worshiped
counsellor	counselor		
crueller	crueler	cruellest	cruelest
jeweller	jeweler		
traveller	traveler		
woollen	woolen		

There are also some words which have a double l in American English, but a single l in British English, for example:

UK	US
appal	appall
enrol	enroll
enthral	enthrall
fulfil	fulfill
instalment	installment
skilful	skillful
thraldom	thralldom
wilful	willful

SAME WORD, DIFFERENT SPELLING

There are also some words that are spelt differently in British and American English that do not fit into any of the above categories, but which are worth noting:

UK	US
annexe	annex
axe	ax
cosy	cozy
grey	gray

UK	US
jewellery	jewelry
mould	mold
moult	molt
plough	plow
sceptic	skeptic
tyre	tire

EXERCISE

The following are all film titles. In brackets after each title is the country where the film originated, either Britain (UK) or America (US). Each title contains a word that is spelt differently in British and American English. Is the spelling of each title correct for the film's country of origin?

- ▶ *Pearl Harbour (US)*
- ▶ *Rumor Has It (US)*
- ▶ *Journey to the Centre of the Earth (US)*
- ▶ *The Time Traveler's Wife (US)*
- ▶ *Analyse This (US)*
- ▶ *Licence to Kill (UK)*
- ▶ *The Color Purple (US)*
- ▶ *The Plowman's Lunch (UK)*
- ▶ *My Favorite Wife (US)*
- ▶ *Charlotte Gray (UK)*

Spellcheckers

Every word-processing package comes with a built-in spellchecker. As you type your document, the spellchecker highlights any word that it suspects may be incorrectly spelt. It does this by comparing the words you type with a list of 'correct' or accepted spellings that is contained within the package. When you type a word that is not in the list, it flags it up as a mistake and, in most cases, offers you a choice of possible 'correct' spellings.

This can be useful but can also be intensely irritating, as words that are perfectly correct are highlighted because they do not appear in the spellchecker's list. This is especially frustrating if you are typing a document with technical or specialist language and a large number of words are not recognized as valid. There are often problems with proper names as well. The name **Eilidh**, for example, which is not uncommon in Scotland (it is Gaelic for **Helen**), is not recognized by the spellchecker in my word processor, and it is therefore underlined with a red squiggly line and a selection of alternatives are offered to me: **Eolith, Elide, Eyelid, Exiled** and **Eoliths**.

To get round this you can add the 'incorrect' word to your spellchecker's dictionary, so the spellchecker will recognize that it is correct and not a typing mistake. You also have the option of turning the spellchecker off, which you may or may not want to do.

Spellcheckers also perform useful corrections on the common errors that occur in typing. If you do a lot of word processing, you will probably be aware of the mistakes that you make regularly, for example 'teh' for 'the', 'ot' for 'to' or 'liek' for 'like'. These are typing rather than spelling mistakes, and typically involve swapping two letters round. Your spellchecker will recognize these as mistakes and correct them automatically as you type, which is useful and time-saving. Spellcheckers will also highlight errors that are harder to spot, such as the the repetition of a word – as in the previous clause, where I have deliberately typed 'the' twice.

All in all, the spellchecker provides a useful service to the writer. But it is not infallible.

As mentioned earlier, a spellchecker works by comparing the typed word with a list of acceptable spellings. These lists can vary in quality, and even the best can still have a mistake in it. So if your spellchecker's word list contains the incorrect 'liason' instead of the correct 'liaison', you will be led to believe that 'liason' is the correct spelling. (This is a true-life example which, happily, has now been corrected.)

The way the spellchecker works is also the cause of its greatest drawback. Because it works by recognizing 'correct' words, as long as a word is in the spellchecker's list of words that are correct, it will consider the word to be correct, even if the word being used is completely wrong in that context. For example, if you type 'hoards of people', the spellchecker is perfectly happy with it: 'hoards', 'of' and 'people' are all correctly spelt, so there's no problem. Unfortunately, there is a problem and that problem is that the correct word is not 'hoards' but its homophone 'hordes': *hordes of people*. If you type 'a horde of Viking treasure' there is no fuzzy red line to warn you that you have used the wrong word: it should be *a hoard of Viking treasure*.

Because of the large number of homophones in English (and you can read more about these in Chapter 8), there is a lot of potential for using the wrong word when you write, and your spellchecker won't let you know as long as you have typed a word that it recognizes.

This is not to say that spellcheckers are useless, because that is certainly not the case. As I have already said, they are a useful tool for correcting slips of the finger like 'teh' and 'taht' and for making you think about what you are typing.

But they should not be used in isolation. You should *always* read carefully what you have written. Pay particular attention to words that are close in spelling or pronunciation to other words. Ask yourself if you really meant to write 'a counsel official will call'. Should it perhaps be 'a council official will call'? Read your writing over again and check any words you are unsure of in a dictionary. That way you can reduce the chance of being led astray by your spellchecker, and increase the chance of producing writing that is both correctly spelt and perfectly correct.

The following passage contains a number of mistakes that have not been identified by my spellchecker. Can you find them?

Four his birthday, Rory (he's hour sun) asked if he could take some friends two the zoo. This did seem like good idea to his farther and me. I am quiet lazy and the thought of having a hoard of screaming boys in the house, praying games and making allot of noise, did nought appeal to me at all. On the day of this birthday we took ate little boys to Edinburgh Zoo. They had a ball. They loved the guerrillas, the flamencos and the cheaters. After we had been to see all the animals, we went to a restaurant for tee. The children had stake and chips, and I had too large biers!

Insight

If you would like to read a whole poem on the dangers of spellcheckers, you can go to www.bios.niu.edu/zar/poem.pdf and read 'Candidate for a Pullet Surprise' by Professor Jerrold H Zar.

Exercise

If you have a paper dictionary, see how quickly you can find the entries for the words in the following list. Just look at the word quickly and then try to find it in the book. Or, if you have a volunteer to help you, get them to read the word out loud to you, and then look it up in the dictionary. This is a good way to get used to consulting a dictionary, and it should help reinforce the correct spelling of some tricky words.

- ▶ aficionado
- ▶ bachelor
- ▶ cigarette
- ▶ diarrhoea
- ▶ embarrass

- *fluorescent*
- *inoculate*
- *lieutenant*
- *mischievous*
- *obsess*
- *occasion*
- *paraffin*
- *pneumonia*
- *psychiatry*
- *rhythm*
- *silhouette*
- *unnecessary*
- *veterinary*

10-question diagnostic test

1. *What does the word **dictionary** mean?*
2. *What has research shown about why people use a dictionary?*
3. *Which word can you use to check if an online dictionary is British or American?*
4. *Which is the American spelling: **license** or **licence**?*
5. *Which is the American spelling: **practise** or **practice**?*
6. *How does American English spell words that end in **our**?*
7. *How does American English spell words that end in **re**?*
8. *How does American English spell words that end in **ogue**?*
9. *How does American English spell words that contain **ae**?*
10. *How does American English spell words that contain **oe**?*

10 THINGS TO REMEMBER

1 *A dictionary is essential.*

2 *A small or middle-sized dictionary will be large enough for everyday use.*

3 *Look inside the dictionary before buying to make sure you can read it without trouble.*

4 *Check to see if the dictionary gives you all the spelling forms you would like.*

5 *An online dictionary is fine as long as you use a reputable one.*

6 *Avoid online dictionaries that can be edited by anyone.*

7 *Make sure you choose a British dictionary and not an American one.*

8 *Spellcheckers are useful for finding common typing errors.*

9 *Always check what you have written by reading it through.*

10 *Never rely on a spellchecker alone.*

11

What are you doing here?

In this chapter you will learn:
- *how English borrows words from many other languages*
- *how language continuously develops and changes as our society diversifies*
- *how the internet helps to bring new foreign words into English.*

English has always been peculiarly welcoming to words from other languages, a fact which probably reflects its own diverse origins (see Chapter 2 for a brief history of English). Unlike French, for example, which has *L'Académie française* (The French Academy) to advise on vocabulary, usage and grammar, English has been shaped by its use alone. There is no official body that rules on whether a word is 'proper' English or not. This aversion to rule-making is reflected by British dictionaries of English. All British lexicographers (the people who write dictionaries) would argue in favour of 'descriptive' rather than 'prescriptive' dictionaries. By this they mean that the purpose of a dictionary is not to dictate how the language *should* be used, but to reflect on how it actually *is* used.

Historically, some conservative writers and commentators have objected to what they see as a dilution or debasement of the English language by foreign borrowings. But this is a difficult argument to sustain. At what point in English's history would it be right to say that this is the 'pure' English? The Old English of the writer of *Beowulf*? The Middle English of Chaucer? The Early Modern English of Shakespeare? The Modern English of Samuel

Johnson's dictionary? Even the English of the 1980s would be inadequate for the way we live now – there would be no *website*, *laptop* or *MP3 player*.

Languages develop and change because human reality develops and changes: new words are coined, existing words take on new senses, old words drop out of use, some words become unacceptable, and other words become standard. These changes in language reflect changes in the real world: new inventions, new technology, new food, new music, and new sensibilities. English absorbs and adapts the vocabulary it needs to keep up with the times, and often this vocabulary comes in the shape of loan words from other languages. Over time these words become naturalized into English, with English pronunciations and plurals, and eventually they are so firmly embedded in the language that people forget they were ever considered to be strange and new.

Lists of words from other languages

You will see below that many of the words we consider to be part of the basic vocabulary of English started off as anything but.

WORDS FROM LATIN

All the words in the English language that are from Latin would fill a book bigger than this one, so the following list contains only a tiny number of them. When you find yourself with access to a dictionary that shows word origins and you have half an hour to spare, have a look at a few entries at random and be prepared to marvel at how many are from Latin.

abbreviate	act	allude
ability	add	ambiguous
absent	admit	ambivalent
accelerate	affect	appeal
accuse	age	army

art
artifice
attest
aural
avuncular

balance
base
beast
biannual
biceps
biennial
bonus
bottle
bovine
branch

cabin
cage
calendar
callous
callus
cancer
candelabrum
captain
case
castle
census
century
choir
classify
coast
collaborate
concise
condition
configuration
consensus
copy

correspondent
corroborate
cortex
council
cross
cure

data
decimal
decorate
delineate
delude
dementia
denote
describe
desert
diary
digit
diva
divorce
doctor

eagle
ebullient
educate
effect
elegant
elicit
elude
emigrate
emotion
error
et cetera
example
excuse
exceed
exercise
exert

exfoliate
exposition

face
fact
fair
false
family
favour
ferment
fervent
fiction
focus
follicle
form
front
fury

germ
gestate
glue
govern
gradual

habitat
hesitate
hibernate
hospital

identity
illusion
imaginary
imbecile
immigrate
imminent
immoral
impetus
imply

important	nepotism	puerile
inane	nominate	pugnacious
incredible	notion	
inept	numerous	quality
infant		quantity
innovate	object	quiet
intelligence	obnoxious	quote
intricate	obsolete	
	omen	radius
janitor	occasion	rapid
jealous	opera	reason
joy	oral	recuperate
junior	orbit	relax
		respect
kennel	pagan	rose
kitchen	parent	rural
	part	
labour	peel	sacred
language	pencil	salary
legal	people	scene
letter	perpetrate	science
library	persecute	script
litigation	personal	second
local	picture	secret
	pigeon	sense
machine	place	sex
major	poison	site
mention	possible	sound
merit	potential	story
military	precede	stupid
minor	precise	sudden
money	preposterous	superficial
	prevent	superfluous
narrate	prey	support
nation	prime	
native	proceed	table
necessary	promise	tax
negative	public	temple

tenacious	tractor	valid
tenor	tradition	vapour
terminal	transport	vegetable
territory	turn	ventilate
timid		verb
tint	ultimate	vest
tolerate	ultramarine	victory
tonsil	urban	villa
torment	urine	violent
tortoise	utility	vocation
total		vulgar

WORDS FROM GREEK

The impact of Greek on English has been considerable, so the list below is just a selection to illustrate its influence.

academy	catholic	iris
acrobat	climax	irony
adamant	cycle	
agony		kaleidoscope
alphabet	democracy	
amphibious	diabetes	magic
androgynous	disc	menopause
angel	drastic	metre
anthology	dyspepsia	monarch
apocalypse		
apostle	echo	nautical
arithmetic	ecology	nomad
asthma	epidemic	
	ethic	orphan
basilica	euthanasia	oxygen
bible		
bomb	genesis	panic
		paraphrase
canon	hierarchy	perimeter
cardiac		phenomenon
catalogue	idiot	phobia

planet	sceptic	theme
pneumonia	scorpion	therm
protein	sperm	
psyche	strategy	xenophobia
pyramid	synagogue	
	synergy	zodiac
sarcasm	system	

WORDS FROM MODERN GREEK

bouzouki	ouzo	tavern
feta	pitta	tzatziki
halloumi	retsina	
moussaka	taramasalata	

Insight

The words from Modern Greek reflect the way in which most
English speakers encounter the language – as tourists who are
enjoying a holiday in Greece, listening to the music, eating
the food and sampling the local alcohol.

WORDS FROM FRENCH

After Latin, French has been by far the greatest contributor to
English vocabulary. Once again, this is just a small selection of the
words brought into English through French.

ace	blame	cease
achieve	blanch	change
admire	blancmange	city
air	blasé	close
amuse	brave	common
assist	budget	company
avalanche		contest
	cadet	cord
bail	café	country
bank	calm	course
beauty	career	
beef	carrot	damage

deliver
descend
dessert
develop
duty

effort
egalitarian
empire
employ
enter
escape
expert

fame
feast
female
final
forest
fry

garden
genre
gentle
grand
group
guitar

herb
hotel
human
hurt

immerse
impose
ink

jail
jewel

juggle
justice

large
legend
lemon
locket
lure

malign
march
marry
medal
menu
mercy
monster
multiply

neat
negligible
noble
note
number

obey
observe
oil
oppose
order

page
parade
pardon
party
pay
peace
perfume
picnic
pity

plain
plumage
point
police
poor
power
practical
profit
pray

quay
queue
quit

raisin
receive
repeat
return
romantic

saint
save
scarce
sentence
simple
sombre
sorbet
stage
suppose

task
taste
tiger
tremble
trouble
tutu

uncle
unique

use	vessel	wafer
	volume	
veil	vulture	zero
vent		zest

WORDS FROM OLD NORSE

aloft	freckle	raft
anger		raise
ankle	gap	ransack
awe	gasp	reindeer
awkward	girth	rid
	gosling	rotten
bag	gust	
bait		saga
ball	haggle	scare
bang		scathe
bark	ill	scrap
berserk		seem
birth	keel	skate (fish)
blether	kettle	skill
bulk	kirk	skin
		skirt
cake	leg	sky
cast	lift	slaughter
clip	litmus	sleight
club	loan	sleuth
crook	loose	sly
crawl	low	snub
		stagger
daze	meek	steak
dirt	mire	stern (boat)
	mistake	
eddy		tang
egg	oaf	tarn
	odd	tern
flat		tether
flit	race	their

them	ugly	whirl
they		whisker
thrive	wand	window
troll	want	wing
trust	weak	

Insight

Old Norse words came into English with the Viking invasions. Rather like those from Anglo-Saxon, Old Norse words tend to be short, and relate to the practical and physical world. The pronoun **they** is Old Norse, while **I**, **he**, **she** and **we** are all from Anglo-Saxon.

WORDS FROM NORWEGIAN

axel	floe	mogul
dollop	gunnera	quisling
dump	kraken	sild
fjord	lemming	ski
flare	minke	slalom

WORDS FROM SWEDISH

Aga	feldspar	ombudsman
angstrom	freesia	smörgåsbord
dahlia	gravlax	tungsten
eider	mink	

WORDS FROM FINNISH

sauna

WORDS FROM DANISH

bohrium
Lego
narwhal

WORDS FROM ICELANDIC

geyser

WORDS FROM GERMAN

abseil
affenpinscher

berg
blitz
bratwurst

cobalt

dachshund
delicatessen
Doberman
doppelganger

edelweiss
ersatz

-fest
foosball
frankfurter

glockenspiel

hinterland

Kaiser
kaput
kindergarten
kirsch

Liebfraumilch

marzipan

Nazi
nickel

pinscher
poodle
poltergeist
pretzel

quartz

realpolitik
Reich
Rottweiler
rucksack

sauerkraut
schadenfreude
schnapps
schnauzer
spitz
spritzer
strudel

umlaut

waltz
wanderlust
Weimaraner
wolfram
wunderkind

zeitgeist
zinc
zither

Insight

Many dog breeds of German origin are now well established in Britain and elsewhere. The **Weimaraner**, **Rottweiler** and **pinscher** take their names from places, while the **Doberman** is named after a famous dog breeder. The **dachshund** is the 'badger dog', the **affenpinscher** is the 'monkey pinscher' and the **poodle** is the 'splashing dog'.

WORDS FROM ITALIAN

adagio
alfresco
allegro
antic
arsenal

balcony
ballerina
balloon
ballot
bandit
bimbo
broccoli
buffalo

cameo
cannelloni
cappuccino
carnival
ciabatta
citadel
concert
confetti
crescendo

dilettante
ditto
duel

falsetto
fiasco
finale

ghetto
graffiti
grotto

impresario
incognito
influenza
isolate

lagoon
lasagne
lava
legato
lottery

manage
manifesto
minestrone
miniature
motto
mozzarella

oboe
opera

panini
paparazzi
pasta
piano
picturesque
pizza
portfolio

profile

quarantine

ravioli
regatta

scenario
semolina
soda
solo
sonata
sonnet
soprano
squadron
staccato
stiletto

tempo
tombola
trampoline
trill
trombone
tuba

umbrella

vendetta
vista
volcano

Insight

The Italian words in English illustrate the areas for which
the country and its people are renowned: music, art and, in
(Contd)

recent years, food. All musical instructions are in Italian, for example **allegro**, **legato** and **staccato**.

WORDS FROM DUTCH

blink	foist	pump
bluff	freight	
blunderbuss	frolic	quack (doctor)
boom		
booze	gherkin	roster
boss	gin	
brandy	golf	skate
brawl		sketch
bully	hanker	sledge
bundle	holster	slim
bumpkin		slurp
bung	iceberg	snack
		snoop
cockatoo	kink	splinter
coleslaw		split
cookie	landscape	spook
cruise	loiter	
	luck	tattoo (military)
deck		trek
decoy	maelstrom	trigger
dock	meerkat	
domineer		veld
dope	pickle	
drill	pinkie	waffle
	pit (fruit stone)	wagon
easel	plug	walrus
etch	polder	
	poppycock	yacht

WORDS FROM SPANISH

alligator	armada	barbecue
alpaca	armadillo	barracuda
anchovy	avocado	bolero

bonanza
bronco
burrito

cafeteria
cannibal
canoe
canyon
cargo
chocolate
chorizo
cigar
cockroach
condor
corral
coyote
crimson

embargo

flamenco

guerrilla

hurricane

iguana
incommunicado

jalapeño

lariat
lasso
llama

macho
mosquito
mustang

nacho

oregano

paella
papaya
patio
plaza
poncho
potato
puma

ranch
renegade
rodeo
rumba

salsa
savanna
sherry
sierra
siesta
silo
sombrero
stampede

taco
tango
tequila
tobacco
tomato
tornado
tortilla
tuna

vamoose
vigilante

WORDS FROM PORTUGUESE

albacore
albatross
albino
amah
auto-da-fé

banana
bossa nova

capoeira
cashew

caste
cobra
creole

dodo

emu

flamingo

jaguar

junk (boat)

lambada

macaw
mandarin
mango
mangrove
maraca
marmalade
molasses

negro	samba	veranda
	sargasso	
pagoda		yam
palaver	tapioca	
piranha	teak	

WORDS FROM HEBREW

Bar Mitzvah	kibbutz	shekel
Bat Mitzvah		shibboleth
behemoth	matzo	
	menorah	Talmud
cherub		Torah
	rabbi	
hallelujah		yeshiva
	seraph	
kabbalah	shalom	

WORDS FROM YIDDISH

bagel	mazeltov	schmooze
bubkes		schmuck
	nosh	schmutter
chutzpah		schnozzle
	pastrami	shtoom
gazump		
	schlep	tush
kvetch	schmaltz	
	schmo	yarmulke

....
Insight

Yiddish, the language spoken by Jewish people throughout
the world, is of Germanic origin, with words from many
other languages. Most of the Yiddish words in English are
used in informal contexts, and many contain the distinctive
sh sound, such as **schlep** and **schnozzle**. Others relate to
Jewish culture, such as **yarmulke** and **bagel**.
....

WORDS FROM RUSSIAN

agitprop
apparatchik

babushka
balalaika
blini or bliny
Bolshevik
borscht or borsch

commissar
cosmonaut

dacha
duma or douma

glasnost
Gulag

intelligentsia

Kalashnikov
kolkhoz
kremlin

mammoth
matroyshka
Menshevik

-nik
nomenklatura

perestroika
pogrom
Politburo

rouble or ruble

samizdat
samovar
shaman
soviet
Sputnik
Stakhanovite
steppe

tovarich
tsar or czar
tsarina or czarina
troika

vodka

WORDS FROM CZECH

haček
pilsner

pistol
polka

robot
Semtex

WORDS FROM ARABIC

alchemy
alcohol
alkali
almanac

djellaba

emir

fakir
falafel
fatwa

ghoul
giraffe

hadj
halal
harem
hashish
harissa
henna
hookah

imam

jihad

kasbah
kebab

loofah

madrasa
mohair

nadir
niqab

orange

sheikh
sofa

tahini
tarragon

yashmak

zenith
zircon

WORDS FROM SANSKRIT

ashram

chakra

juggernaut
jute

Kama sutra

maharishi
mahatma
mantra

nirvana

suttee
swastika

yoga

WORDS FROM PERSIAN

attar
ayatollah

baksheesh
bazaar

caravan

divan

hijab
houri

jackal

peri
pyjamas

seersucker
sherbet

taffeta

WORDS FROM TURKISH

aga

baklava
bey
bulgur

caftan

coffee

dolman

kilim
kiosk
kismet

macramé

pasha

turban

yoghurt

WORDS FROM HINDI

ayah

balti

bandana
bangle
basmati

bhindi
blighty
bungalow

cheetah
chintz
chit
chutney
cummerbund

dekko
dinghy
dungaree

ghee
guru
gymkhana

jalfrezi
jungle

kedgeree

loot

maharajah
masala
mehndi

naan
nawab

pakora
pundit
puttee

raita
raj
rana
rani

samosa
sari
shampoo
sitar
swami

table
tandoori
thug
tikka
toddy
tom-tom

veranda

wallah

WORDS FROM URDU

aloo

begum
bhuna
biryani
burka

doosra

izzat

kameez
khaki

purdah

rogan josh
rupee

sepoy
shalwar

WORDS FROM CHINESE

cha
cheongsam
chi
chop suey
chow mein

dim sum

fan-tan
feng shui

ginseng
gung-ho

hoisin

kowtow
kumquat
kung fu

lapsang souchong
lychee

mah-jong

pak choi

sampan

shar-Pei
shih tzu

t'ai chi

wok
won ton

yang
yin

WORDS FROM JAPANESE

adzuki
akita
anime

basho
bento
bonsai

geisha
ginkgo

haiku
hara-kiri

honcho

ikebana

kabuki
kamikaze
karaoke
kimono
koi
kudzu

manga
mikado
mirin
miso
mizuna

nashi
netsuke
Noh

obi
origami

ramen
rickshaw
rikishi
ronin

sake or saki
samurai
sashimi
satsuma
shiatsu
shiitake

Shinto
shogun
soba
soya
sudoku
sukiyaki
sumo
sushi

tempura
teppan-yaki
teriyaki
tofu
tsunami
tycoon

udo
udon

wasabi

yakitori

Zen

WORDS FROM AFRIKAANS

aardvark
apartheid

dorp
ringhals

rooibos

WORDS FROM SWAHILI

bwana	kitenge	safari
dengue	Kwanzaa	
jambo	piri-piri	

WORDS FROM OTHER AFRICAN LANGUAGES

baobab	dashiki	vuvuzela
calypso	marimba	zebra
chimpanzee	mojo	zombie
cola	okra	

WORDS FROM AUSTRALIAN ABORIGINAL LANGUAGES

barramundi	jackaroo	wallaby
billabong	joey	wallaroo
boomerang		willy-willy
budgerigar	kangaroo	witchetty
bunyip	koala	wombat
	kookaburra	
coolabah	kylie	yabber
didgeridoo	nulla-nulla	
dingo	numbat	

WORDS FROM MAORI

haka	kiwi	tiki
kia-ora	moa	

WORDS FROM HAWAIIAN

aloha	luau	ukulele
hula-hula	muu-muu	wiki

WORDS FROM NATIVE AMERICAN LANGUAGES

chipmunk	moose	terrapin
hickory	opossum	toboggan
moccasin	racoon	totem

WORDS FROM INUIT

anorak
igloo
kayak

This is by no means a complete list of the languages that have contributed words to English over the centuries. The range of vocabulary is astonishing and without this borrowing from other tongues, English would not be the multi-layered and fascinating language it is today. And it is this adaptability that has helped to ensure its place as *the* global language.

Exercise

One of the most fertile areas for English borrowing nowadays is food and drink. Many of the loan words that have come into the language in recent years have been dishes and ingredients from around the world. This borrowing comes about in two ways. Firstly, English speakers travel abroad for holidays and work, and experience the cuisine of the countries they visit. And secondly, recent immigrants often open or work in restaurants that serve the food from their homelands, giving it exposure to the English-speaking population.

Many of the words in the lists above are drinks, dishes and ingredients from other countries. Which other food words can you think of that came into English from other languages and are now firmly established in our vocabulary?

10-question diagnostic test

1 *Which language does 'dachshund' come from?*
2 *Which language does 'emu' come from?*
3 *Which language does 'safari' come from?*
4 *Which language does 'pistol' come from?*
5 *Which language does 'anorak' come from?*
6 *Which language does 'kowtow' come from?*
7 *Which language does 'bangle' come from?*
8 *Which language does 'coffee' come from?*
9 *Which language does 'cookie' come from?*
10 *Which language does 'sofa' come from?*

10 THINGS TO REMEMBER

1 *English has borrowed thousands of words from dozens of languages.*

2 *Words from other languages are called loan words.*

3 *When a loan word becomes so established in the language that it is no longer thought of as being 'foreign', we say that it is 'naturalized'.*

4 *The language that has contributed most words to English is Latin.*

5 *The next biggest contributor is French, mostly in the 300 years following the Norman Conquest.*

6 *Old Norse words came into English when the Vikings invaded and then settled.*

7 *The spread of the British Empire accounts for many of the words from India, North America and Canada, Africa, Australia and New Zealand.*

8 *English speakers travelling abroad help to popularize foreign words that relate to culture, food, dress and music.*

9 *Immigrants into Britain bring their own words that are then absorbed into English.*

10 *Nowadays the internet helps to bring new foreign words into English.*

12

A spell of fun

In this chapter you will learn:
* *that word- and letter-related games are fun and help with spelling practice*
* *about crosswords, word searches, Scrabble® and other internet and multi-media word and letter games*
* *about spelling bees and the part they play in American education.*

Now you have done all the hard work, and you are feeling more confident about your ability to spell correctly, how about a little word-related fun? There are lots of spelling and word games to play, in all sorts of formats.

Crosswords

The crossword has come a long way since the publication of its first known example in English, in the *New York World* newspaper in 1913, when it was called a 'word-cross'. It is believed the very first crossword ever published was in 1890 in an Italian magazine, in a four-by-four grid, with clues for horizontal and vertical answers.

The basic format of the crossword is a square grid with some shaded boxes to mark the end of a word. Other boxes are numbered to show where a word should be inserted. There is a numbered clue for each word to be inserted, whether it is horizontally (known as 'across') or vertically (known as 'down').

There can be many different types of clues. The most basic is the synonym, where the answer is another word for the clue given, for example 'mountain ash' for 'rowan' or 'Christian festival' for 'Easter'. The number of letters in the word is shown in brackets after the clue.

Clues are often in the form of anagrams, where you have to rearrange the letters of the clue or part of the clue to make the answer, for example 'wines for pigs' is 'swine'.

Other clues consist of two words, both of which share a synonym, for example 'speak fast' for 'express' ('express' means both 'to speak' and 'fast') or 'downright thin' for 'sheer' ('sheer' means both 'downright' and 'thin').

Nowadays every British newspaper and general magazine has at least one crossword in each edition. These crosswords are often also available to play online, so if you haven't had a chance to pick up your daily paper, you don't have to miss out on your daily crossword. Most newspapers also publish paperback collections of their crosswords for enthusiasts.

Levels of difficulty vary from paper to paper, from the completely straightforward to the most fiendish of the cryptic crosswords.

If you are a crossword virgin, you might like to have a look at some of the numerous crossword magazines available, some of which are even pocket-sized. If you have a handheld games console such as a Nintendo DS or Game Boy, there are crossword packages available for these.

Insight

The jocular name given to a crossword enthusiast is **cruciverbalist**, which comes from Latin *crux* meaning 'cross' and *verbum* meaning 'word'. Despite its archaic appearance, this word was only coined in the twentieth century.

Exercise

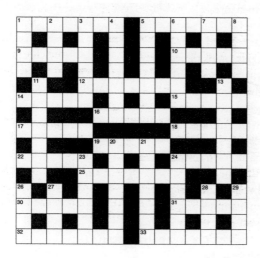

Across

1 a boil (7)
5 a view of an exhibition before it opens officially (7)
9 not easily bent (5)
10 to move slowly and quietly (5)
12 eternal (7)
14 to mention (5)
15 the joint in the arm (5)
16 to make up for doing something wrong (5)
17 to take by force (5)
18 an even number below ten (5)
19 in a strange way (5)
22 to take without permission (5)
24 a small juicy fruit (5)
25 a raging fire (7)
30 a Welsh dog (5)
31 to give knowledge to (5)
32 to treat without care (7)
33 to rush about angrily (7)

(Contd)

EXERCISE

Down

1 a land measure (4)
2 a symbol (4)
3 to make beloved (6)
4 able to pay one's debts (7)
5 a decorative design (7)
6 to forgive (6)
7 a thought (4)
8 to clean by rubbing (4)
11 a souvenir (7)
13 food made from fermented milk (7)
20 openly disobedient (7)
21 a dog bred for hunting (7)
23 to make a connection with (6)
24 the lowest part of something (6)
26 a small image on a computer screen (4)
27 an amphibian (4)
28 a Buddhist priest (4)
29 a covering for the foot (4)

Word searches

A word search is a grid of letters that contains a number of words within it, usually on a theme, for example vegetables, Christmas, inventors, and so on. The words to be found are listed beside the grid. These words can appear vertically, horizontally or diagonally in the grid, and can be written either forwards or backwards. The aim is to find all the words listed. Sometimes there is an extra challenge to find all the unused letters and then rearrange them into another, often related, word.

Many newspapers and magazines contain word searches, as do puzzle magazines. There are also dedicated word search magazines available.

Exercise

All the words below are connected with spelling, reading and writing.
Can you find them all in the word search grid? They can be positioned
vertically, horizontally or diagonally, and can read backwards or forwards.
When you have found all the words, there should be 19 unused letters
remaining. Can you rearrange these letters into a phrase connected with
the subject of this book? (There is a clue at the end of the list.)

ACCENT
ACUTE
ANGLO-NORMAN
APOSTROPHE
BOOK
CAPITAL LETTER
CHECK
CIRCUMFLEX
CONSONANT
COPY
COVER
CURRICULUM VITAE
DICTIONARY
FONT
FULL STOP
GRAVE
GREAT VOWEL SHIFT
HOMOPHONE
KEY
LETTER GAME
LOAN WORD
LOOK
MAIL
MISSPELT
MNEMONIC
PAPER
PEN
PREFIX

(Contd)

PRINTING PRESS
PROOFREADING
READ
ROOT
RULES
RUNE
SAY
SCRABBLE
SMALL LETTER
SPELLCHECKER
SPELLING REFORM
STANDARDIZE
STUDY
SUFFIX
TILDE
TIP
VOWEL
WRITE

Clue: it is a three-word phrase

C	S	P	E	L	L	I	N	G	R	E	F	O	R	M
I	S	V	R	E	K	C	E	H	C	L	L	E	P	S
N	E	Z	I	D	R	A	D	N	A	T	S	I	E	O
O	R	C	A	P	I	T	A	L	L	E	T	T	E	R
M	P	U	G	A	Y	F	S	E	D	L	I	T	P	E
E	G	R	S	P	R	U	N	E	E	R	E	E	R	T
N	N	R	C	E	A	L	U	P	W	T	N	O	F	T
M	I	I	R	R	N	L	S	G	K	L	O	I	I	E
P	T	C	A	P	O	S	T	R	O	P	H	E	N	L
R	N	U	B	P	I	T	U	A	O	S	P	I	N	L
O	I	L	B	M	T	O	D	V	L	A	O	A	L	L
O	R	U	L	L	C	P	Y	E	K	Y	M	K	O	A
F	P	M	E	A	I	Y	W	V	T	R	O	C	A	M
R	E	V	O	C	D	O	O	N	O	R	H	E	N	S
E	S	I	L	U	V	R	E	N	S	W	E	H	W	P
A	E	T	I	T	P	C	O	P	Y	U	E	C	O	R
D	L	A	A	E	C	L	K	O	O	B	F	L	R	E
I	U	E	M	A	G	R	E	T	T	E	L	F	D	F
N	R	M	T	N	A	N	O	S	N	O	C	E	I	I
G	R	E	A	D	C	I	R	C	U	M	F	L	E	X

Letter games

I am using the term 'letter games' to describe a variety of games that are based on making words out of individual letters.

SCRABBLE®

This is the original letter game and it is still going strong more than 70 years after its invention by an American architect called Alfred Mosher Butts.

Insight
It took a few years and a variety of names – including Lexico, Alph and Criss-Crosswords – before the ubiquitous letter game finally become Scrabble®, and was copyrighted and registered as a trademark in December 1948.

It is a game for two or more players. Each player starts with seven randomly-chosen letter tiles with which they have to try to create a word on a special board. There are 100 tiles in total, 98 of which have a letter with an assigned value, for example A is worth one point and Z is worth ten points. Two tiles are blank and can be used in place of any letter. Players take turns to make their words, scoring points according to the letters used and the position on the board. After each play they must pick more titles so that they always have seven on their rack. When all the tiles have been taken, and no further play is possible, each player's score is added up and the winner is the one with the most points.

Insight
Scrabble® inventor Alfred Mosher Butts made the decision about how many tiles each letter should have by counting the occurrences of each letter of the alphabet on the front page of the *New York Times*.

Scrabble® is usually played on a board, but other, more high-tech, formats are available: there is an Internet Scrabble® Club where

you can play online against other people; there is also a Scrabble®
application on the social-networking site Facebook; Scrabble®
packages are also available for Nintendo DS, Game Boy, Nintendo
Wii and even for the iPhone and iPod.

Insight

The word 'kwyjibo', as played by Bart Simpson and defined
by him as 'a big, dumb, balding North American ape with no
chin', is not a valid Scrabble® word.

LEXULOUS

This is a game very similar to Scrabble® that can be played online
only. It is available on its own website, or in an application on
Facebook.

WORD CHALLENGE

This game, available to play through a website or as a Facebook
application, is another variation on the theme of making words out of
a number of letters. In this one, you are given six letters and then have
a limited amount of time to find all the words that can be made from
these letters. It is easy to play and, I must say, curiously addictive.

BOOKWORM

This is a computer game or an online game that requires players to
create words out of adjacent letters in a grid: the longer the word,
the higher the score given. When you use a letter, another letter
drops into the top of the grid. For added excitement, every so often
one of the letters bursts into flames and, unless you use it in a word
pretty quickly, the fire spreads and destroys the entire grid, and the
game is over.

A LOW-TECH VERSION

If you are a Luddite or there's been a power cut but you have
candles, you can still play a version of these letter games. Each

player has a pen and paper. Look in your dictionary (another good reason to have a printed copy!) and choose a longish word (at least eight letters, say). Now see how many smaller words you can make from those letters. Use your dictionary to settle the resulting arguments.

COUNTDOWN

If you are feeling really lazy, lie on your settee and watch *Countdown* on Channel 4. The contestants have nine letters from which to make the longest word they can, and there's even a nine-letter anagram to solve, known as the '*Countdown* Conundrum'.

Spelling bees

The spelling bee, in which a competitor (usually a child) is asked to spell a number of words out loud, is a cultural phenomenon that has not really taken off in Britain. Yet spelling bees play a large part in American education, where there are competitions between classmates and classes within schools, and then between students from different schools and districts. The ultimate aim is to qualify for the final of the National Spelling Bee, which is open to children from all over the States. This competition is televised and was the subject of a highly acclaimed documentary film in 2002, *Spellbound*. The spelling bee is well established in the American psyche, and many comedy shows have based episodes around one of these competitions, for example *The Simpsons*, *Family Guy*, *South Park*, *My Name is Earl* and *Roseanne*.

If you want to try a spelling bee for yourself, you could use the spelling list in Chapter 6 to test your family and friends. Of course, now that you have worked your way through this book, it would be unfair for you to take part, so you had better be the question master.

Insight

This kind of bee is not connected to the honey-making buzzing insect. Its origin is uncertain but it has been suggested that it comes from a dialect word *bean*, meaning 'neighbourly help'.

10-question diagnostic test

1 When was the first English crossword published?
2 By which name was the crossword originally known?
3 In which country was the first crossword published?
4 What is the jocular name for a crossword fan?
5 Who invented Scrabble®?
6 How many tiles are there in Scrabble®?
7 How many letters are there in a rack?
8 How much is the letter Z worth?
9 How many blank tiles are there?
10 What is the name of the film about the US National Spelling Bee?

10 THINGS TO REMEMBER

1 *Playing word games can help you improve your spelling.*

2 *There is a word game to suit every age and every kind of speller.*

3 *You can play word and letter games in newspapers and magazines.*

4 *You can play word games in books.*

5 *You can play word games online and against other people if you want.*

6 *You can play word games on your mobile phone.*

7 *You can play word games on your MP3 player.*

8 *You can play word games on your games console.*

9 *You can play word games with nothing more than a pencil and a piece of paper.*

10 *You can even lie back and watch other people play word games on TV!*

Glossary

abbreviation An abbreviation is a shortened form of a word, either with some letters missing, eg Dr for Doctor, or with each word represented by its first letter, eg RAF for Royal Air Force.

acronym An acronym is word created from the first letters of a group of words, eg NATO for North Atlantic Treaty Organization. An acronym is different from an abbreviation in that it is pronounced as a word, not as a series of letters, so NATO is an acronym because it is pronounced 'nay-to' and RAF is an abbreviation because it is pronounced as three individual letters, 'R - A - F'.

active In grammar, an active verb is one where the subject (shown in bold) performs the action, eg *The **janitor** painted the wall*; ***Dad** baked the birthday cake*; ***Eve** scored the goal of the tournament* (see also **passive**).

adjective An adjective is a word that is used to describe someone or something, eg **jolly**, **honest** and **Dutch**.

adverb An adverb is a word that is used to add meaning to a verb, adjective or another adverb, eg **very**, **unusually** and **often**.

affix An affix is another name for a prefix or a suffix.

anagram An anagram is a word with letters that can be rearranged into another word, eg **decimal**, **claimed** and **declaim** are all anagrams of **medical**.

antonym An antonym is a word that means the opposite of another word, eg **living** is the antonym of **dead** (see also **synonym**).

common noun A common noun is a noun that does not refer to a particular person, thing or place, eg **woman, mountain** and **rainforest**. Common nouns do not start with a capital letter (see also **proper noun**).

comparative An adjective or adverb is comparative when it is being used to describe something that is *more* than something else, eg **smellier, more interesting** and **farther** (see also **positive** and **superlative**).

conjunction A conjunction is a word that links two words, eg *bells **and** whistles, wine **or** beer* and *tired **but** happy*.

consonant A consonant is a letter of the alphabet that is not a vowel, that is every letter except for **a, e, i, o** and **u**.

first person plural In grammar, the first person plural is the person who is speaking or writing, along with other people, and this is shown by the use of **we**, eg *We were in Tenerife for a week; We are moving house.*

first person singular In grammar, the first person singular is the person who is speaking or writing and this is shown by the use of **I**, eg *I have been on holiday; I wish it would stop raining.*

future tense The future tense is the tense that describes events that have not happened yet, eg *Mary **will be** at the party; I **will give** you the book tomorrow*. In English the future tense is made by the verb **will** and the basic form of the verb, eg **be** and **give**.

headword In a dictionary, the headword is the word shown prominently at the start of an entry. Dictionaries are arranged alphabetically by headword.

homophone A homophone is a word that sounds the same as another word although it means something different or is spelt differently, or both. For example, **fritter** (to waste) and **fritter** (fried food) are homophones (same spelling but different meanings), as are **camomile** and **chamomile** (same meaning but different spellings), and **flower** and **flour** (different spellings and different meanings).

irregular If a noun, verb, adjective or adverb is irregular, it does not follow the normal rules when it becomes plural, changes to show tense, or becomes comparative or superlative.

long vowel In English, a long vowel is one that is elongated when it is pronounced. The following words all have long vowels: **train, play, feed, field, please, ski, night, time, bone, moan, show, tube** and **blew**.

noun A noun is a word that is used to name something, eg **car, elephant** and **happiness**.

object In grammar, the object of a verb or preposition is the person or thing affected by it, eg *The dog chased the cyclist*; *Give me that*; *I waved to her* (see also **subject**).

passive In grammar, a passive verb is one where the subject undergoes the action of the verb, instead of performing it. In the following sentences the subject is shown in bold: *The wall was painted by the janitor*; *The birthday cake was baked by Dad*; *The goal of the tournament was scored by Eve* (see also **active**).

past participle The past participle is the form of a verb that is used with another verb to show that something happened in the past, eg *I have **eaten** sushi*; *He has never **forgiven** her*; *The girls had already **gone** home*.

past tense The past tense is the tense that describes events that have already happened, eg *Jessie **fell** in the street*; *My father **was** in the Air Force*.

person In grammar, person is a form of a word relating to whether it is the person who is speaking or writing (see **first person singular** and **first person plural**), the person who is being spoken or written to (see **second person**) or the person who is being spoken or written about (see **third person singular** and **third person plural**).

phoneme A phoneme is the smallest unit of sound that has a meaning in a language, eg the sounds 't', 'b' or 'sh'.

plural A plural is a form of a noun or verb that shows that more than one person or thing is meant, eg **tattoos** or **have** in the sentence *Both girls* **have tattoos**.

positive An adjective or adverb is positive when it is not being used to compare with something else, eg **smelly**, **interesting** and **far** (see also **comparative** and **superlative**).

prefix A prefix is a letter or group of letters added to the beginning of a word to add to or change its meaning, eg **anti-**, **e-** and **re-**.

preposition A preposition is a word put before a noun or pronoun to show its relation to another word, eg *the book* **on** *the table; he kicked the ball* **into** *the crowd; I am going away* **for** *a month.*

present participle *The* present participle is the form of a verb that ends with **-ing**, that shows that something is happening now, in the present, eg *I am* **talking** *to Mary; You are* **sitting** *on my scarf; The bus is* **coming**.

present tense The present tense is the tense that describes events that are happening now, eg *George* **is** *very busy; I* **am drinking** *a cup of tea.*

pronoun A pronoun is word that is used in place of a noun, eg **I**, **she** and **they**.

proper noun A proper noun is a noun that refers to a particular person, thing or place, eg **Cheryl, Mount Everest** and **Amazonia**. Proper nouns start with a capital letter.

regular If a noun, verb, adjective or adverb is regular, it follows the normal rules when it becomes plural, changes to show tense, or becomes comparative or superlative.

second person In grammar, the second person is the person or people that the speaker or writer is talking to and this is shown by the use of **you**, eg *You are late*; *You will all need to have a bath this evening*. Unlike some languages, English does not have different words for the second person singular and the second person plural: **you** is used whether it means one person or a hundred.

short vowel In English, a short vowel is one that is not elongated when it is pronounced and is usually (although not always) represented by a single vowel in the written word. The following words all have short vowels: **cat, pen, dig, mop, cup, put, deaf, caught, through** and **should**.

silent If a letter in a word is silent, you do not pronounce it when you say the word, eg the letter **e** in **place**, **b** in **debt**, **p** in **psychic** and **g** in **gnome**.

singular A singular is a form of a noun or verb that shows that one person or thing is meant, eg **a dachshund** or **has** in the sentence *My sister has a dachshund*.

stress Stress is extra emphasis put on a syllable or word when you are speaking, eg the second syllable in the word **refreshment** (re-**fresh**-ment).

subject In grammar, the subject is the person or thing doing the action in a sentence, eg *John has measles*; *The Titanic sank*; *I am going out* (see also **object**).

suffix A suffix is a letter or group of letters added to the end of a word to add to or change its meaning, eg -ness, -ed and -est.

superlative An adjective or adverb is superlative when it is being used to describe something that has the *most* of a certain quality, eg **smelliest, most interesting** and **farthest** (see also **positive** and **comparative**).

syllable A syllable is a word or a part of a word that is said with one breath, eg **mouse** has one syllable, **cheetah** has two syllables ('cheet' and 'ah'), **crocodile** has three syllables ('croc' and 'o' and 'dile'), **alligator** has four syllables ('all' and 'i' and 'gat' and 'or'), **hippopotamus** has five syllables ('hip' and 'po' and 'pot' and 'a' and 'mus'), and so on.

synonym A synonym is a word that means the same as another word, eg **happy** is a synonym of **glad** (see also **antonym**).

tense The tense of a verb is the form it takes in order to show when an action occurs, eg in the present (*It **is** Monday today*), the past (*It **was** Sunday yesterday*) or the future (*It **will be** Tuesday tomorrow*).

third person plural In grammar, the third person plural is the people or things that the speaker or writer is talking about and this is shown by the use of **they** or by the name of the people or things, eg *They left the house in a terrible mess*; *The teachers are going on strike next month*; *Elephants are supposed to have good memories*. In these sentences **they**, **the teachers** and **elephants** are all third person plural.

third person singular In grammar, the third person singular is the person or thing that the speaker or writer is talking about and this is shown by the use of **he, she** or **it**, or by the name of the person or thing, eg *He can never remember his dreams*; *The dog ran away last night*; *David is playing in the* *park just now*. In these sentences **he**, **the dog** and **David** are all third person singular.

....

verb A verb is a word that describes what someone or something is doing, eg **carry**, **snore** and **have**.

....

vowel A vowel is any one of the letters **a**, **e**, **i**, **o** and **u**.

....

Recommended websites

Dictionaries

www.chambersharrap.co.uk
www.collinslanguage.com
www.oup.co.uk
www.thefreedictionary.com (look for the definitions that come
from *The Collins Dictionary*, which are British English)

Spelling reform

www.spellingsociety.org

This website lists the arguments in favour of spelling reform.

Word games

www.isc.ro (the Internet Scrabble® Club)
www.lexulous.com
www.playfish.com (look for the 'Word Challenge' game)
www.popcap.com (look for the 'Bookworm' game)

Answers to exercises

Chapter 1

(page 6)

Résumé

To whom it may concern:

I want to apply for the job that I saw in the paper. I can type really quickly with one finger and do some accounting. I think I am good on the phone and I know I am a people person. People really seem to respond well to me: certain men and all the ladies. I know my spelling is not too good but I find that I often can get a job through my personality.

My salary is open so we can discuss what you want to pay me and what you think I am worth.

I can start immediately. Thank you in advance for your answer.

Hopefully I am your best applicant so far.

Sincerely

Bryan

PS: Because my résumé is a bit short, below is a picture of me.

(page 6)

10-question diagnostic test

1	*I care about spelling.*	**6**	*Yes*
2	*Yes*	**7**	*No*
3	*Yes*	**8**	*Yes*
4	*Yes*	**9**	*Yes*
5	*Yes*	**10**	*Yes*

If you have given any of the above answers to the questions, then you should carry on reading this book!

Chapter 2

(page 14)

1 *The* **rain** *in* **Spain** *falls* **mainly** *on the* **plain.**
2 *I will need* **red thread** *to finish sewing this* **bedspread,** *she* **said.**
3 *Have you* **heard** *that* absurd Birdie *Song that they always play at weddings?*
4 *I love to* **run** *along the beach before the* **sun** *is* **up.**
5 *The* **chief reason** *for being* **here** *is to drink all your* **beer.**

(page 15)

1 *Did you* **receive** *the* **parcel** *I* **sent?** *It was the DVD of* **Sex** *and the* **City.**
2 *He was feeling* **especially anxious** *because he knew that the* **crucial** *interview with the* **National** *Trust was* **scheduled** *for the next day.*
3 *It's no* **fun** *when you have a* **cough** *and you can't get any medicine because the* **pharmacy** *closed at* **half** *past one.*

4 *Trying to explain the pension* scheme *to you is* like talking *to a* brick *wall.*

5 *The* days *passed by in a* haze *of* booze *and parties.*

(page 16)

1 *Everyone* knows *that George Clooney is a* handsome *man.*

2 *In days of old,* knights *may have been bold, but they still carried their* swords *everywhere.*

3 *Last* Wednesday *we went to London to see the* sights. *My favourites were Nelson's* Column *and the River* Thames.

4 *Tying a* knot *in your* handkerchief *is supposed to help you remember things.*

5 *When the* tsunami *hit the* island, *a huge wave destroyed the houses, leaving* debris *everywhere.*

6 *I would* like smoked *salmon and a glass of* champagne.

7 *Dame* Margot *Fonteyn earned great* fame *as a* ballet *dancer.*

8 *I had* pneumonia *the* whole *of last* autumn *and it was* Christmas *before I was completely better.*

9 *It's none of your* damn business *how I spend my money!*

(page 19)

10-question diagnostic test

1 *in the third century* AD

2 *the Angles, the Saxons and the Jutes*

3 *Celtic languages*

4 *Anglo-Saxon and Old English*

5 *the arrival of Christianity brought new words from Latin*

6 *with the arrival of the Vikings*

7 *Old Norman*

8 *the Great Vowel Shift*

9 *the first book was printed in English*

10 *'thorn' and 'eth'*

Chapter 3

(page 25)

Word	Word contained
beggar	egg
committee	mitt
desperate	era
eulogy	log
extrovert	rover
peculiar	liar
prairie	air
prominent	mine
soliloquy	lilo
wholly	holly

(page 28)

10-question diagnostic test

1 *read*
2 *we recognize the shape*
3 *a notebook, an address book, a mobile phone*
4 *a word within a word*
5 *connecting words*
6 *breaking words down into smaller pieces*
7 *check it*
8 *ask someone else to check it*
9 *think about it and then check it in a dictionary*
10 *read, say, cover, write, check*

Chapter 4

(page 60)

1 *I like to take* **bunches** *of grapes when I visit my* **uncles** *in hospital.*
2 *The* **berries** *had frozen on the* **branches** *of the holly* **bushes** *in our* **gardens.**
3 *He had put* **shampoos, soaps,** *face* **cloths and aftershaves** *on the* **shelves** *in the* **bathroom.**
4 *The* **bailiffs** *and their* **wives** *brought us tea* **caddies** *and* **avocados.**
5 *Did you get the* **memos** *I sent about the windows for the new* **embassies?**
6 *Please leave your* **scarves, gloves** *and* **umbrellas** *in the hall.*
7 *Lynne is studying the* **phenomena** *of the missing* **giraffes.**
8 *Those* **companies** *are famous for treating their* **staff** *appallingly.*
9 *No* **zoos** *in this country have* **cheetahs, rhinos, emus, zebras, baboons** *and* **chimpanzees** *living in the same* **enclosures.**
10 *The* **biographies** *of famous war* **heroes** *form the* **bases** *for the* **films.**

(page 61)
blacker, blackest
yummier, yummiest
redder, reddest
limper, limpest
drearier, dreariest
tweer, tweest
feyer, feyest
fiercer, fiercest
hipper, hippest
severer, severest

(page 61)
prays
defends
shampoos

blitzes
carries
shanghais
fusses
laughs
coaches
fixes

(page 62)
dubbing
feeling
noting
propelling
skipping
kneeing
gassing

frolicking
marring
boogieing

(page 62)
contrived
plodded
concealed
swooped
appalled
topped
frolicked
bussed
poked
partied

(page 63)

whiteness	faddy	shield
merriment	prettily	brief
guitarist	wreckage	weird
councillor	helpless	pierce
snaky	developer	species
gentleness	appreciative	hygiene
knowledgeable		heinous
capably	(page 65)	ceiling
trespasser	field	achieve
classifiable	seize	fierce
frolicky	grief	receipt
namedropper	sheila	either
grievance	thief	niece
humorous	protein	
	caffeine	

(page 67)

1 *Who ever thought it would be interesting to* **televise** *parliament? Correct.*

2 *We need to* **devize** *a new sales strategy. Incorrect: it should be* **devise**.

3 *She asked me to* **supervise** *her students while she was on holiday. Correct.*

4 *America and China both need to* **compromise** *if there is to be an agreement on climate change. Correct.*

5 *I ended up trying to* **prize** *the drawer open with a kitchen knife. Incorrect: it should be* **prise**.

6 *He plans to* **disguise** *himself and sneak into his ex-girlfriend's wedding. Correct.*

7 *In the new year I intend to* **exercize** *three times a week. Incorrect: it should be* **exercise**.

8 *Do you think it would be expensive to* **advertise** *on the radio? Correct.*

9 *The idea is to turn up at his office and* **surprize** *him. Incorrect: it should be* **surprise**.

10 *I* **prize** *my independence too much to get married and settle down. Correct.*

(page 68)

10-question diagnostic test

1 *es*
2 *s and x*
3 *echoes, heroes, potatoes and tomatoes*
4 *k*
5 *antennae*
6 *two Sassenachs*
7 *develop*
8 *mislaid*
9 *ee*
10 *despise*

Chapter 5

(page 74)

This **Christmas I** am going to the **wedding** of my friends Douglas and **Angela**. It will be held in a **hotel** in the **south side** of Glasgow, and I expect to see a lot of people I have not seen since **last year**. The whole wedding will be taking place in the **hotel,** and the **minister** is coming up from Ayrshire to perform the **ceremony**. The weather forecast on the BBC last night said that there is a good chance there will be snow on Christmas **Day**. That would be lovely for the photographs but I just hope that all the **guests** will be able to get here. Will I have to wear my **wellies** under my dress?

(page 82)

The start of a new year is traditionally the time to **turn over** a new leaf and make resolutions about the things you will do better or **give up**. These often relate to **health issues** like smoking, diet and exercise. I plan to **take up** running again with the aim of competing in a **ten-kilometre** race next May. It is for women only. Last year almost **15,000** people **took part**. I **sometimes** find it hard to make myself go out on a cold winter's night, but I know I'll feel more **up for it** when the days get longer in the **run-up** to the race. A few of my **well-off** friends are members of the posh gym near here but I have never enjoyed exercising **indoors**.

(page 87)

10-question diagnostic text

1 *a.m.*
2 *to show possession and to show where a letter is missing*
3 *when it is for a small letter, e.g.* graffiti *has two* **f**'s
4 a *and* e
5 a, e *and* o
6 n
7 c
8 e
9 a, o *and* u
10 i *and* e

Chapter 6

(page 100)

10-question diagnostic test

1 *the double* f *and the single* t
2 *the unusual combination of three vowels in a row*
3 *the unusual combination of two* u*'s in a row*
4 *the single* f *where you might expect a double* f
5 *the silent* b
6 **fridge** *has a* d *so people think* **refrigerator** *should have one as well*

7 *the single l where you might expect a double l*
8 *the single s and the double c*
9 **restaurant** *has an* **n**, *so people think* **restaurateur** *should have one as well*
10 **impress** *has a double* **s**, *so people think* **impresario** *should have a double* **s** *as well*

___

Chapter 7

(page 110)

hydrophobia	fear of water
astrology	study of stars
omnivore	one who feeds on everything
polyhedron	geometric solid with many sides
neophilia	love of new things
bilingual	having two languages
aquiferous	containing water
monotheism	belief in one god
rhinoscope	examination of the nose
patricide	murder of the father

(page 111)

self-writing	autograph
study of animals	zoology
pulling action	traction
related to blood	haemic
device for measuring time	chronometer
government by women	gynarchy
inflammation of the nose	rhinitis
related to the name of the father	patronymic
disease of the mind	psychopathy
related to having two feet	bipedal

(page III)

10-question diagnostic test

1 *homeo-*
2 *iso-*
3 *ortho-*
4 *dys-*
5 *-tomy*
6 *-ism*
7 *-ways*
8 *crypt*
9 *mort*
10 *vac*

Chapter 8

(page 171)

The school athletics **team** recently took part in a national
competition. It was **quite** an adventure. The school **principal** asked
for parents to help out and I volunteered. I was the only one with
a clean driving **licence** so I ended up driving the minibus, which
had been leant to us by the local **council**. We also had to **raise** the
money needed to pay for the trip. We did this by having a 'festive
fair' and the Women's **Guild** held a **bazaar** for us in the **nave** of
the church. A local businessman gave us a **cheque** for £200.
All the **profits** went into our competition trip fund.

Meanwhile the children each had to **practise** for their own event.
The competition itself was a **great** success. Although they were up
against some schools who were much more experienced than they
were, our pupils were not at all **fazed** by it. The organizers even
complimented us on their attitude and enthusiasm. The **heroine** of

the squad was Helen, who won the 100 **metres** and also ran the final leg of the relay race, where she recovered from a poor **baton** change to finish in second **place**.

Our team came home with no fewer than seven **medals**.

(page 172)

10-question diagnostic test

1 *a word that sounds the same as another word*
2 *camomile and chamomile (and various others in the chapter)*
3 *fritter (to waste) and fritter (the fried food) (and various others in the chapter)*
4 *flour and flower (and various others in the chapter)*
5 *Scotch whisky*
6 *'Gentlemen Prefer Blondes' (but gentlemen marry brunettes)*
7 *advice*
8 *practise*
9 *you do not want to lose them*
10 *you have to catch your breath*

Chapter 9

(page 180)

1 *Are your friends actually **real, Lynne?** (really)*
2 *He's not as tall as the chap I **met re**cently. (metre)*
3 *It's time to **reig**nite the debate about the monarchy. (reign)*
4 *Ivan has a country cottage on the Rive**r Ural.** (rural)*
5 *If she's not certain about something, Ava gue**sses.** (vague)*
6 *Has **evil lain** within his heart all this time? (villain)*
7 *You should give this culinary cu**stom a ch**ance. (stomach)*
8 *She sa**ves tigers** from poachers, the few that remain. (vestige)*

9 *Put the can in the locker between eight and ten. (ninth)*
10 *I don't think Ivor* **Novello** *wrote books. (novel)*

(page 180)

10-question diagnostic test

1 *a way of remembering something*
2 *Greek*
3 *mindful*
4 *Richard of York gave battle in vain*
5 *every good boy deserves favour*
6 *Cabal*
7 i *before* e *except after* c
8 *full-word mnemonic*
9 *partial mnemonic*
10 *initial mnemonic*

Chapter 10

(page 195)

Pearl Harbour (US) Incorrect: the US spelling is 'harbor'

Rumor Has It (US) Correct US spelling: the UK spelling is 'rumour'

Journey to the Centre of the Earth (US) Incorrect: the US spelling is 'center'

The Time Traveler's Wife (US) Correct US spelling: the UK spelling is 'traveller'

Analyse This (US) Incorrect: the US spelling is 'analyze'

Licence to Kill (UK) Correct UK spelling: the US spelling is 'license'

The Color Purple (US) Correct US spelling: the UK spelling is 'colour'

The Plowman's Lunch (UK) Incorrect: the UK spelling is 'ploughman's'

My Favorite Wife (US) Correct US spelling: the UK spelling is 'favourite'

Charlotte Gray (UK) Correct: trick question, I'm afraid. The woman's name is Gray, so it's always spelt with an **a**!

(page 198)

For his birthday, Rory (he's **our son**) asked if he could take some friends **to** the zoo. This did seem like good idea to his **father** and me. I am **quite** lazy and the thought of having a **horde** of screaming boys in the house, **playing** games and making **a lot** of noise, did **not** appeal to me at all. On the day of **his** birthday we took **eight** little boys to Edinburgh Zoo. They had a ball. They loved the **gorillas**, the **flamingos** and the **cheetahs**. After we had been to see all the animals, we went to a restaurant for **tea**. The children had **steak** and chips, and I had **two** large **beers**!

(page 199)

10-question diagnostic test

1 *a collection of words*
2 *the main reason is to check spelling*
3 *grey*
4 *license*
5 *practice*
6 **or**
7 **er**
8 **og**
9 **e**
10 **e**

Chapter 11

(page 221)

10-question diagnostic test

1 *German*
2 *Portuguese*
3 *Swahili*
4 *Czech*
5 *Inuit*

6 *Chinese*
7 *Hindi*
8 *Turkish*
9 *Dutch*
10 *Arabic*

Chapter 12

(page 225)

Crossword

(page 227)

Wordsearch

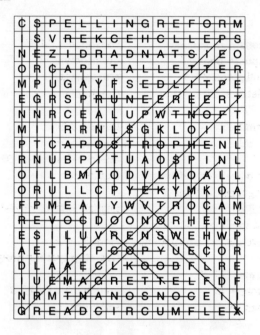

The unused letters spell the phrase: IMPROVE YOUR SPELLING

(page 232)

10-question diagnostic test

1 *1913*
2 *Word-cross*
3 *Italy*
4 *cruciverbalist*
5 *Alfred Mosher Butts*

6 *100*
7 *seven*
8 *ten points*
9 *two*
10 *'Spellbound'*

Index

Notes

Notes

Notes

Notes

Notes

Notes

Notes

Notes

Notes

Notes

Notes

Notes

Image credits

Front cover: © G. P. Kidd/Photographer's Choice RF/Getty Images